THE

Faygo

BOOK

THE

Faygo

BOOK

Joe Grimm

A PAINTED TURTLE BOOK

DETROIT, MICHIGAN

© 2018 by Wayne State University Press, Detroit, Michigan 48201.
All rights reserved. No part of this book may be reproduced without
formal permission. Manufactured in the United States of America.

ISBN 978-0-8143-4585-6 (paperback)
ISBN 978-0-8143-4586-3 (e-book)

Library of Congress Control Number: 2018943986

Wayne State University Press
Leonard N. Simons Building
4809 Woodward Avenue
Detroit, Michigan 48201–1309

Visit us online at wsupress.wayne.edu

Dedicated to the Feigenson family,

Faygo, and the people of Detroit,

who love their pop

Contents

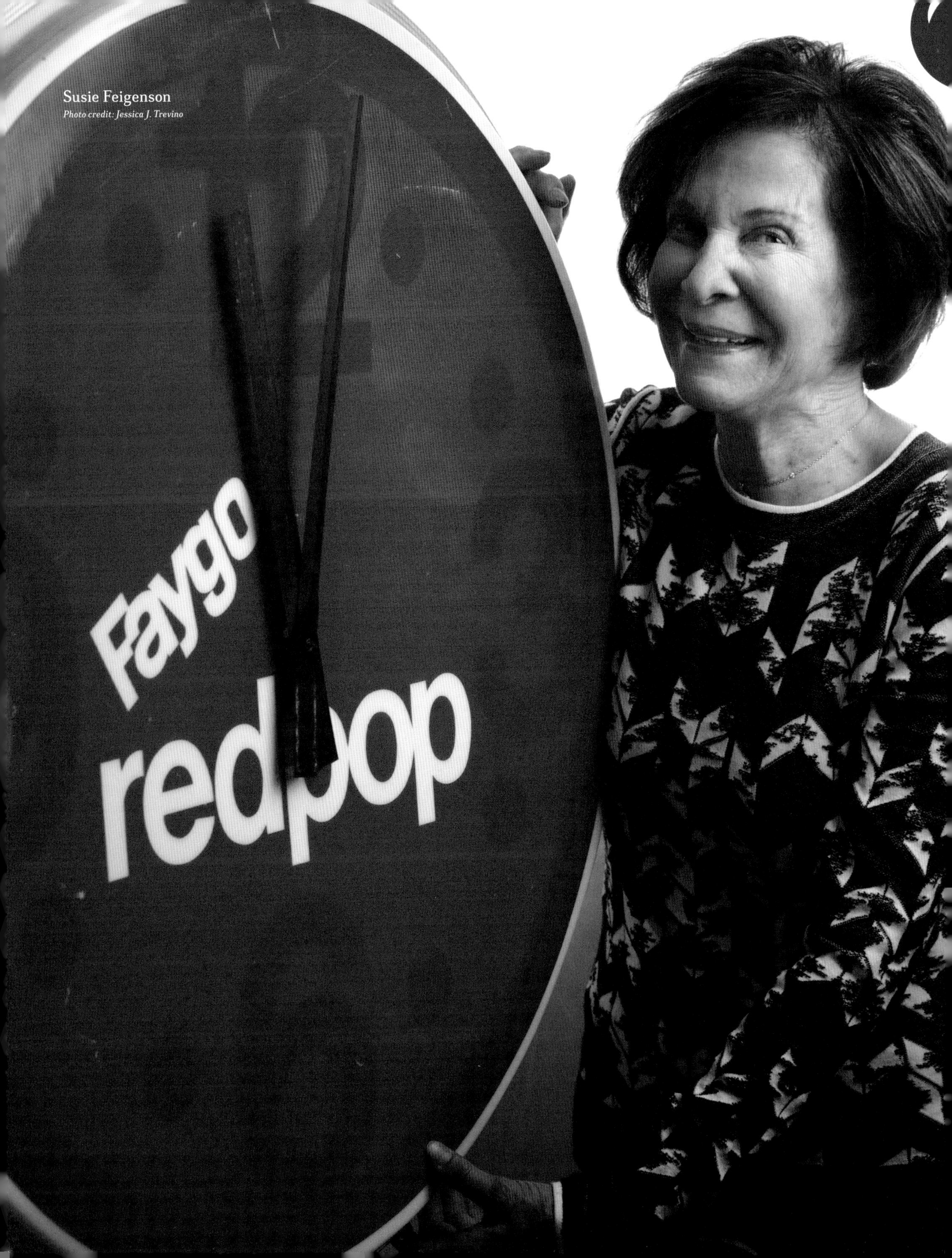

Susie Feigenson
Photo credit: Jessica J. Trevino

Foreword

Having taught high school for forty-two years and my last name being Feigenson, I've often thought I had red ink running in one arm and Redpop in the other. Indeed, this book came about because a former student, Alex Scharg, who knew my family background, hooked me up with his former journalism teacher at Michigan State University, Joe Grimm, who wanted to tell the story. Thanks to both, the history of Faygo Beverages has come to be.

Faygo is more than a product. It is a family history, to be sure, but more, its story reflects a city and a spirit. Associating Faygo with Detroit is as natural as sunshine and summer. When Garrison Keillor came to the Fox Theatre to do a segment of his *Prairie Home Companion* radio hour, he led the audience in singing the Faygo commercial: "Remember when you were a kid? Well, part

of you still is. And that's why we make Faygo. Faygo remembers . . ."

On a much more personal level, I remember. For, to me, the history of Faygo is so much of what I remember about my father, Philip Feigenson. I remember my father teasing me after I had stirred all the carbonation out of my glass. "Do you know how long it takes me to put all those bubbles in?" he asked. And, of course, I cried and said I would never do it again. I remember that when he came home at night, I would snuggle my nose into his shirt to see what flavor he smelled like that day. Grape? Rock & Rye? Root beer? And I remember working at the plant the summer of 1967 and seeing the lines of tanks on Gratiot after the riots. Later that day, I found a note on his desk with names and amounts of money he had loaned to employees.

When National Public Radio had a daily sponsor program, my message read, "In loving memory of Philip Feigenson, whose life exemplified optimism, generosity, and integrity." That's how he ran his life; that's how he ran Faygo. This is dedicated to the memory of a great businessman and father.

—Susie Feigenson

Preface

Detroit has bonds with many institutions, but few are as old, as tight, or as fizzy as the city's bond with Faygo.

These Faygo stories, which began shortly after 1900, when the automobile was still young, will tickle the taste buds and memories of Detroiters and Faygo lovers everywhere.

The Faygo Book is not a chronology. It is a social history that tells about Faygo and its hometown, a tumultuous industry, immigrant brothers who put their stamp on the American Century, and the people who love what the Feigenson family did and made. The book is organized by topic, not by date. For instance, you will find the long-running stories of sweeteners, bottling, and Faygo commercials in chapters of their own, rather than sprinkled about, like sugar, over Faygo's more than one hundred years. This lets us peer into different facets of the story.

This is not a company history, either. It is not the product of lengthy interviews with Faygo executives or an examination of company archives, earnings reports, memos, and ledgers. The door remains open for Faygo to tell its story in its own way. The focus here is on the dreams and values of the Feigensons, who created the company and led it for nearly eight decades. It explores how the company forged a bond with Detroit and Detroiters, who saw Faygo as much more than a pop company. The book explores how National Beverage Corp. has sustained Faygo values in the more than thirty years since the Feigensons sold the company. Above all, this book is intended to be a story about people and loyalty.

At the heart of the book is Susie Feigenson, granddaughter of Ben Feigenson, who founded the company with his older brother, Perry. In several long interviews, she shared family memories and stories. She also shared articles, images, and artifacts that have been in her family's homes since the 1980s. Her brother Ben, named after their grandfather, also provided some long-distance help. Susie's love for her family, Faygo, and Detroit, as well as her editing, touch every page. In these pages, Susie Feigenson has more than kept up her role as keeper of the Feigenson flame.

Other people who helped, but who are not credited in the story, include Alex Scharg, who, as Susie Feigenson explained in the foreword, connected us after I mentioned my interest in telling the Faygo story. Without that, this book could not have happened.

Ed Golick, Tim Kiska, and Bill Kubota helped with the story of Faygo's groundbreaking TV advertising. The long connection between Faygo, the Michigan State University marching band, and "Remember When You Were a Kid" was helped by trombonist Adam Mackay (another of my students at MSU), Chad Sanders, Jeremy Steele, and Bob Gould.

Ed Deeb told how, as a youngster working in his father's store, he remembered stocking Faygo, and April Barbee told the story of Faygo-branded cupcakes. Songwriter, guitarist, author, and professor Brian Bowe connected me to Steve Miller, author of *Juggalo: Insane Clown Posse and the World They Made.*

Keith Wunderlich, author of *Vernor's Ginger Ale,* helped clarify the Vernors-Faygo collaboration.

Norma Powell, who works at Campbell Ewald and explores Detroit on her Redpop Bike, introduced me to others in the advertising business, including Lew Baker and Michelle Rossow.

This Faygo story is based on the work of dozens of newspaper, magazine, broadcast, and online writers, reporters, and photographers. Collectively, their contributions show how journalism really can be the first draft of history. Hui Hua Chua, collections and user support librarian and journalism liaison at the Michigan State University Libraries, unlocked these resources. More than one hundred books and articles that went into the book are at listed in the Sources section.

Many articles came from the *Detroit Free Press.* Former *Free Press* photo editor Jessica J. Trevino took great care with the photographs in the book. Former *Free Press* assistant graphics editor Martha Thierry created the graphics. Kathy Kieliszewski, photo and video director at the newspaper, arranged for permission to use several wonderful photographs.

Two online archives in particular were of great help. One was the archive of the *Detroit Jewish News* (1942–) and the *Jewish Chronicle* (1916–1951). This resource, covering more than one hundred years, is available because of the William Davidson Digital Archive of Jewish Detroit History at www.djnfoundation.org. It was the brainchild of publisher Arthur Horwitz.

The archive of the Associated Food and Petroleum Dealers publication, the *Food Dealer,* going back to 1965, is available online http://afpdonline.org/publications/#. It is a trove of information about Detroit's food and beverage industry. Especially helpful to this project was a regular feature about Faygo written by Mort Feigenson in the late 1960s and early 1970s.

Websites, online forums, and social media were invaluable. Many leads showed up in items listed on eBay. Photo-sharing sites such as Flickr and Instagram helped, too. Comments with ideas and sources appeared on Facebook, Twitter, YouTube, and Reddit. The online community was an unpredictable and powerful voice.

The section about television advertising is best told through videos, and links to more than twenty-five are in the Sources section at the end of the book. They will help tell the story much better than I can.

Thanks to all the people at Wayne State University Press who goaded me into doing *The Faygo Book* and then had to make it come out. They include interim director Kathryn Wildfong and her predecessor as director, Jane Ferreyra, as well as Gabe Gloden, former development and community engagement officer. Work in the trenches was done by senior production editor Carrie Downes Teefey; editorial, design, and production manager Kristin Harpster; senior designer Rachel Ross; marketing and sales manager Emily Nowak; and Annie Martin, editor-in-chief. They brought in copyeditor Lindsey Alexander and theBookDesigners.

Why We Love Faygo

Few companies have stuck to cities the way Faygo has stuck to Detroit. To many Detroiters, Faygo simply means Detroit. When people move away, they crave Faygo's sweet memories and sweeter flavors. Mere mention of Faygo uncaps memories, as does the Faygo Boat Song, "Remember When You Were a Kid," which celebrates "comic books and rubber bands, climbing to the treetop, falling down and holding hands, tricycles and Redpop."

There are many reasons for this love affair. One is loyalty. Faygo was born, bred, and is still bottled in Detroit. But this kind of affection is not due simply to origins; it prevails because of Faygo's persistence. That persistence has lasted more than a century.

Auto companies became fat in Detroit and then moved jobs south. Faygo stayed. While Detroit's population started falling off a cliff in the 1950s,

Faygo grew. Bottlers bought and swallowed other bottlers. Faygo's Florida-based owner has kept the company in Detroit.

In an age where corporations have tried to turn local brands into national products without a locus, Faygo has remained Detroit's pop. Its initially limited distribution range kept Faygo a local favorite. Pop did not easily travel distances then, so you could only find it locally. When people saw a Faygo ad in the window of a roadside filling station or convenience store on the way back to Detroit, they knew they were getting closer to home, sweet home. You could almost smell the Redpop. On Gratiot Avenue, where the product has been made since 1935, you really can. Today, having branched out to most states, Faygo holds onto its roots.

For decades, Faygo has been sold by mail order and now online to people who can't get it where they live. A Detroiter who duplicated one of Detroit's other staples, a coney island restaurant, near Las Vegas did not feel he had it right until he negotiated with Faygo for a regular supply of pop. Coney islands built in Los Angeles and Clearwater, Florida, had the same issue: they had to have their Faygo.

Faygo is served at Detroit-themed birthdays and at nuptials as favors and even the wedding cake. This arrangement features Faygo, a Detroit-style coney, Better Made potato chips, and custom labels on the bottles. Cake design by Chad Rabinovitz.

Photo credit: Gabe Gloden

Completing a circle, Just Baked took bakery-inspired Faygo flavors and turned them back into co-branded Faygo cupcakes in 2010.

Detroit radio program director and personality Slacker shows dual loyalty to Faygo and Flint, Michigan.

Photo credit: Slacker/98.7 AMP Radio

Faygo is a marquee attraction at the Detroit Dog Co. in the close-in suburb of Royal Oak. This is how it looked on the first day of the 2017 Arts, Beats and Eats festival. Inside, an upended Faygo vending machine is a base for its counter.

Photo credit: Joe Grimm

Faygo-loving pedal pushers vote with their feet on limited edition Detroit Bikes finished in (clockwise) grape, orange, cotton candy, Redpop, and Moon Mist. *Photo credit: Blake Yard/Detroit Bikes*

Motor City Creations offers candles in Faygo fragrances including Redpop, Rock & Rye, root beer, candy apple, and Moon Mist.
Photo credit: Motor City Creations, LLC

CONSIDER THESE EVENTS, WHICH ALL HAPPENED IN ONE YEAR:

- When a lost two-year-old mixed terrier captured the city's heart, people named the pup after the pop. They called it Faygo.

- In a contest to name the downtown hockey arena for Little Caesars pizza baron Mike Ilitch's Red Wings, "Faygo Dome" was nominated and even featured in a newspaper artist's rendering. It did not win.

- Detroit Bikes, which got rolling in the city's startup boom, introduced limited edition bicycles in Faygo colors: Redpop, grape, cotton candy, orange, and Moon Mist.

- When the horrorcore rap group Insane Clown Posse was told, the night before a concert, not to spray twelve hundred liters of Faygo all over a Lansing venue as it played, it canceled. It did not want to disappoint its Juggalo fans, who expect to be showered with Faygo.

- The news site MLive declared the creation of Faygo Rock & Rye ice cream to be one of the most Michigan stories of the year.

Susie Feigenson, granddaughter of Faygo founder Ben, shows off beauties from her garden with this vase near the front door of her home.

Photo credit: Jessica J. Trevino

We have Faygo-scented candles, Faygo Slurpees and ICEEs, tattoos, and graffiti. Crafters make jewelry out of Faygo bottle caps. We name our pets Faygo, and some people have it as a nickname. There are hundreds of recipes using Faygo for meals, desserts, and cocktails; there are Faygo jellies and jams; and Faygo shows up at weddings. By reversing the Faygo founders' idea of turning cake frosting recipes into soda pop flavors, one bakery created Faygo cupcakes with orange, grape, and Redpop cake and frosting.

While many cities have favorite sons, Detroit is one of the lucky few that has a favorite pop.

Two popular brands have come together in one cup with Redpop, Rock & Rye, and cotton candy 7-Eleven Slurpees. Detroiters consume more Slurpees than any other US market.

Photo credit: 7-Eleven/TPN

From Russia with Frosting

The Faygo story began on the east side of Detroit with two brothers from Russia. Perry and Ben Feigenson were part of a tide of immigrants searching for a new start. A freshening economy in the United States and challenges elsewhere in the world ballooned the number of US arrivals from 3.5 million in the 1890s to 9 million from 1900 to 1910. Immigrants flocked to cities. Detroit was their third most popular destination, after New York and Chicago. Cities offered immigrants all the promise of their new country and the traditions transplanted from the old ones.

In 1900, Detroit had 285,704 people. By 1904, it was 317,591. Perry, 25, and Ben, 23, arrived on this wave. Like some other Jewish immigrants, the Feigensons went into the food and beverage business to feed this population boom. In a 1958 interview, Perry said he started as a baker in Cleveland in 1900 and moved to Detroit in 1905. It was a contentious start. In 1906, a rival baker sued Perry and two others for twenty thousand dollars, equivalent to half a million dollars today. The accuser, Nathan Goldman, charged they had distributed libelous handbills, printed in Hebrew in Cleveland, and had given them to his customers.

The Feigenson brothers began with one horse in 1907 and worked their way up to two. Before they moved out of their first location at Hastings and Benton, their delivery vehicles were burning gasoline instead of hay. *Photo courtesy of the Feigenson family archives*

The *Detroit Free Press* quoted Goldman: "I am not sure that these men had the bills printed, but I know that they are jealous of me because I have been successful. The bill says that my bread is no good, and that I sell loaves three or four weeks old." Goldman's case does not seem to have been a strong one, but the next year Perry was in the bottling business. Looking back on a career that put him on top of the largest independent pop company in the country, Perry said that his experience with bakers' hours made bottlers' hours look better. That led him to try another sugary business: soda pop.

Perry said, "I talked my younger brother, Ben, into joining me, and we called ourselves Feigenson Brothers." They launched their company on November 4, 1907. Their timing was lousy. Twenty days earlier, copper speculators had triggered the Panic of 1907, a worldwide financial crisis. The New York Stock exchange fell almost 50 percent from its high of the year before. Banks turned away customers. New York City nearly went broke.

Perry said he got into the business "by marriage." His sister had married a man who was in the pop business in Cleveland, at Miller-Becker, founded in 1902. Ben, previously a carpenter, had spent a year bottling with that brother-in-law. The Feigenson brothers started their own business at 118 Benton Street. "We had one horse and a wagon, and we washed the bottles by hand. It was hard work, but the saloons and grocery stores were selling a lot of soda pop and we made money,"

Ben told a *Free Press* writer. The brothers had two tubs for washing bottles, pots and pans for mixing concoctions, a siphoning hose for filling, and a hand-capping contraption.

Perry recalled for an unpublished Faygo history by the company's publicist, James P. Chapman, Inc., how well suited horses were for deliveries. The horse learned where to stop along the way. When Perry came out of a saloon without an empty case, the horse noticed and continued to the next one. But there was a drawback, Perry said: "We had a heck of a time when we used the horse for social purposes or for going to the freight depot for a load of supplies because the horse kept stopping in front of every place where we normally made deliveries."

The Feigensons' first flavors were strawberry, fruit punch, and grape, which they based on frosting recipes. They sold eight-ounce bottles for three cents, two for a nickel. "We had a system—we spent one day at the plant bottling the stuff. The next day we went out and sold it," said Perry. A four-page company history written for Faygo's ninetieth anniversary in 1997 said people bought pop only in the summertime then, and the Feigenson brothers spent winters carting bread to the Detroit River for sale in Windsor, Canada, and bringing back fish to sell in Detroit. In 1911, a one-column-by-one-inch ad in the *Free Press* showed the "Feigenson Bros. Bottling Works: Ginger Ale, Mineral Water Etc.," in a frame house at 507 Hastings Street. Hastings was home to Detroit's first Jewish enclave. About six miles to

the north, Henry Ford was manufacturing the best-selling car in the world. People from the South and around the world poured into Detroit from 1910 to 1920. The city's population more than doubled, from 465,766 to 993,678. The Feigensons tore down their plant and built a larger one. They were going to need a better delivery system, too.

In the Chapman interview, Perry Feigenson said the company bought its first truck, from General Motors Corp., in 1912 and that he bought a Ford Model T for himself. Ford did not reciprocate. In those days, pop was sold at stands, and Perry said one stand, across the street from Ford's Model T plant, sold four hundred to five hundred cases of pop a day. Ford, who had strict guidelines for how his workers should eat, bathe, and raise children, ordered the plant gates shut at lunchtime so workers could not buy "belly wash."

But Ford had bigger worries than pop. He kept training men only to lose them. On January 5, 1914, Ford more than doubled wages to five dollars a day and shortened workdays from nine hours to eight. His announcement made front-page news around the world. Ten thousand people were at his Highland Park employment office the next day seeking jobs. Feigenson said that job seekers, many of them immigrants, stood outside the Ford gates waiting for them to open and kept the pop stand in business.

The Feigensons added routes. They hired. Some left, just as workers had left Ford. According to Gary Flinn's *Remembering Flint, Michigan: Stories from the Vehicle City*, two early Feigenson

Perry Feigenson said Faygo's first truck was made by General Motors. GM got into the truck business when William Durant bought the Grabowsky Brothers' Rapid Motor Vehicle Company and the Reliance Motor Co. The truck in the photo of the men in shirtsleeves has a GMC logo, which first appeared on trucks built by Rapid and Reliance in 1912. GM took over manufacturing in 1913. That's Perry with his foot on the front tire. *Photo courtesy of the Feigenson family archives*

employees, Morris Weinstein and Samuel Buckler, founded the Independent Bottling Works in Flint, Michigan. It sold strawberry, grape, and lime pop, as well as Hires Root Beer. Flinn wrote that the company had changed its name to M&S and that its top pops were orange and a strawberry-cherry flavor that people called "Redpop." Decades later, in the 1950s, the company put Redpop on labels. Flinn wrote that the Feigensons initially said the name cheapened the product, but adopted it two years later.

A January 20, 1918, newspaper ad promoting General Motors' exhibit at the Detroit Automobile Show listed the Feigenson Bros. as buyers of another new truck. There would be hundreds

more. The Feigensons grew with Detroit. On New Year's Day 1920, *American Machinist* published this item: "Mich., Detroit – Feigenson Bros., 118 Benton St., has awarded the contract for the construction of a 3 story, 82 x 90 ft. bottling works on Erskine and Beaubie[n] St. Estimated cost, $30,000." Later that year, an ad in *American Bottler* said: "We are now operating in our new plant. We have disposed of the old building and must sell the equipment, which consists of 3 Juniors, 2 Carbonators 1 Miller Hydro Soaker, and 2 filters, all in first class condition. If interested write Feigenson Brothers Company, 600 Beaubien Street, Detroit, Michigan." The Feigensons held an open house at seven thirty p.m. on August

The modern factory, circa 1920. The *Detroit Jewish Chronicle* reported that in the new plant, "The bottle from the time it is cleaned to the time that the bottle is filled and capped does not require the efforts of a single human hand." That's Perry with the cart of cases.

18, 1920. An ad in the *Detroit Jewish Chronicle* declared, "To the public! See a modern plant in operation. See how we make soft drinks. Drinks will be served." Another ad said the new plant had a capacity of seventy-five thousand bottles a day. The Feigensons demonstrated their work at the Michigan State Fair that September. The move roughly coincided with a new name and logo. On October 29, 1920, the Feigenson Brothers Bottling Co. advertised a dozen flavors in the *Detroit Jewish Chronicle* as "Faygo," with the name in curving script. The name fit better on small pop bottles.

During the Great Migration from 1916 to 1930, an estimated 1.6 million people moved from the South to feed northern factories and foundries. Black workers, restricted by deeds from living in most of Detroit, were crowded into the Hastings neighborhood near the Faygo plant. The area become home to Detroit's black population. People called it Black Bottom because of the river-bottom topsoil originally found there, not for the people. It became the economic and cultural backbone for black life in Detroit.

As frustration grew over crowding and substandard housing in the neighborhood, the federal government purchased Faygo's Beaubien property in 1935 for the Brewster-Douglass Housing Projects for low-income African Americans. The brothers took a gamble. They bought a much larger factory about two miles northeast at 3579 Gratiot Avenue. That building had been the Gotfredson Truck Co. plant and before that the Kolb-Gotfredson horse market. Perry recalled, "My brother thought we were overexpanding by making this daring move into a building which was twice as big as the one we had previously occupied, and I won't say that I didn't think he was right, but we made the move."

Faygo's new neighbors in the German and Italian neighborhood included plants for Coca-Cola and Pepsi-Cola and other pop and beer bottlers in what has been called "Pop Alley" and "Soft Drink Row." When Coke and Pepsi moved out of the neighborhood, Faygo connected the buildings, creating a four-hundred-thousand-square-foot complex. This is where Faygo has remained, passed on to sons who, like their fathers, made Faygo for four decades. But the day would come when it looked like Faygo would outgrow Detroit's east side.

Just around the corner from where this delivery truck is parked in 1927, you can see parts of the Faygo logo and the Feigenson Brothers sign. *Photo courtesy of the Feigenson family archives*

Faygo Town

More than 100 years on Detroit's east side

1935-present

3579 Gratiot factory

Woodward

Beaubien

Hastings

Benton

St. Antoine

Division

Alfred

1920-35

Beaubien & Erskine factory

1907-20

Benton & Hastings factory

1905-07

498 St. Antoine bakery

Gratiot

N

1,000 feet

DETROIT

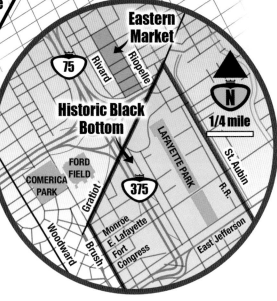

Eastern Market

75

Rivard

Riopelle

Historic Black Bottom

FORD FIELD

COMERICA PARK

Gratiot

375

LAFAYETTE PARK

St. Aubin

R.R.

Woodward

Brush

Monroe

E. Lafayette

Fort

Congress

East Jefferson

N

1/4 mile

Maps and photo illustration by Martha Thierry

Renovations at Faygo headquarters on Gratiot Avenue have long since covered the "Horse Mart" arch that testified to one of the site's early uses. *Photo courtesy of the Feigenson family archives*

It's Pop, Not Soda

Before we go any further into our story, let's get something straight. In Detroit and Michigan, we hold a hand up to show people where things are in the state's Lower Peninsula, we eat coney dogs, and we call carbonated soft drinks "pop." So does this book. A lot of other places, especially in the Midwest, also call it "pop." Contrary to some stories, Faygo did not coin the term. That happened long before the Feigenson brothers were born. The name is a shortened version of soda pop, where the pop sound is made when a pressurized bottle of carbonated soda water is opened.

"Pop" dates back through several kinds of bottles and stoppers to at least 1868–1876. Then, the Mehls Company in Erie, Pennsylvania, embossed its bottles with the words "pop & mineral waters." Around 1910, when the Feigensons' business was still new, other Michigan bottlers were already calling themselves pop companies. However, the bottling industry disdained "pop." The 1913 annual *American Bottler* sneered, "'Pop' means nothing and conveys the idea of a 'cheap and nasty' mixture unfit for human consumption. Reputable manufacturers of carbonated beverages have lifted soda water out of the 'pop' class and hope

soon to eliminate the word from the vernacular." The periodical continued its assault in 1915: "The word 'pop' still creeps into print. Ask the bottlers at your next meeting to help kill it."

Instead, the Feigensons embraced the name and made "pop" more popular. One of Faygo's most successful flavors has been Redpop, an unapologetic rebrand of its original strawberry soda. Early Detroit TV comedian Soupy Sales used to say, "George Washington may be the father of our country, but Faygo is the pop."

An October 24, 1967, advertising column in the *Detroit Free Press* noted that, even after fifty years of complaining, industry leaders still preferred more grown-up–sounding names such as "carbonated beverages." But Detroit ad agency W. B. Doner and Co. developed an ad campaign for Faygo that Doner exec Skip Roberts said would "remind everyone how great pop used to taste and to tell them it was available now in one-calorie flavors." Redpop sales soon climbed 30 percent and overall sales rose 10 percent. Faygo president Mort Feigenson made two observations: "Soft drink bottlers may not like 'pop,' but people do, and a company should let its advertising agency counsel it and not vice versa." A lyric in a Faygo TV commercial asked, "When was the last time you had a good slug of a Redpop?" Mort publicly fretted that "there is a slight danger that we will become known simply as the people who make redpop." But Faygo's in-house *Faygogazette* carried the tagline "The Red Pop People." It was in red ink, of course.

Michigan is Faygo country, and when you are in Faygo country, if you want a carbonated soft drink, you had better ask for pop. Otherwise, you could get thirsty waiting, or you might not get what you expect. The same is true in other places. If you ask a New Yorker for a pop, look out. One exception to the rule is that everyone says "cream soda." Another exception is that Faygo called Frosh, the forerunner of its sugar-free drinks, by the more grown-up name of "soda."

If you sometimes wake up in the morning and don't know exactly where you are, ask the first person you see what they call soft drinks. If they say "soda," you've likely awakened in New England, California, or St. Louis. If they say "Coke," you are in the South, maybe near Coca-Cola headquarters in Atlanta. But if they say "pop," you are likely in a wide band stretching from western Pennsylvania and New York to Oregon and Washington.

Michigan is the pop-locution center of the nation, according to the interactive Pop vs. Soda map by cartographer Alan McConchie. If you like, you can visit the interactive map and vote your preference at http://www.popvssoda.com/. You'll see that Michigan more solidly supports pop than any other place supports any other name. Faygo is one reason why.

Faygo is a proud pop. Its advertising agency, the TMV Group, registered the web address callitpop.com on January 31, 2017, and began a Twitter campaign with the hashtag #callitpop. The campaign was tied into Instagram, Facebook, and billboards and encouraged fans to post videos of themselves taking the pledge to "call it pop." More about advertising campaigns will come later. For now, get used to reading "pop" and we'll get along fine. But, what is pop?

Early Detroit TV comedian Soupy Sales used to say, "George Washington may be the father of our country, but Faygo is the pop."

Alan McConchie/PopVsSoda.com

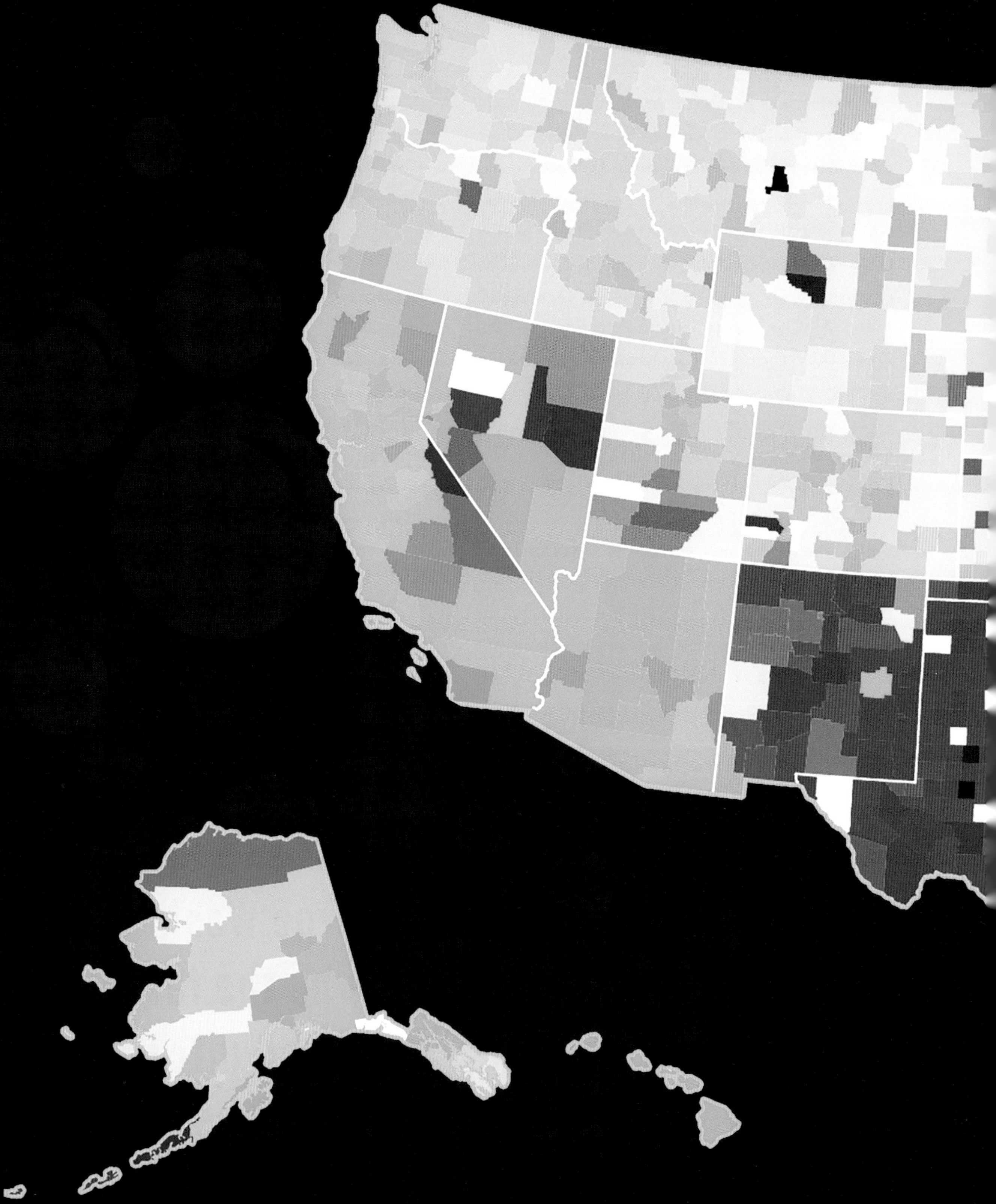

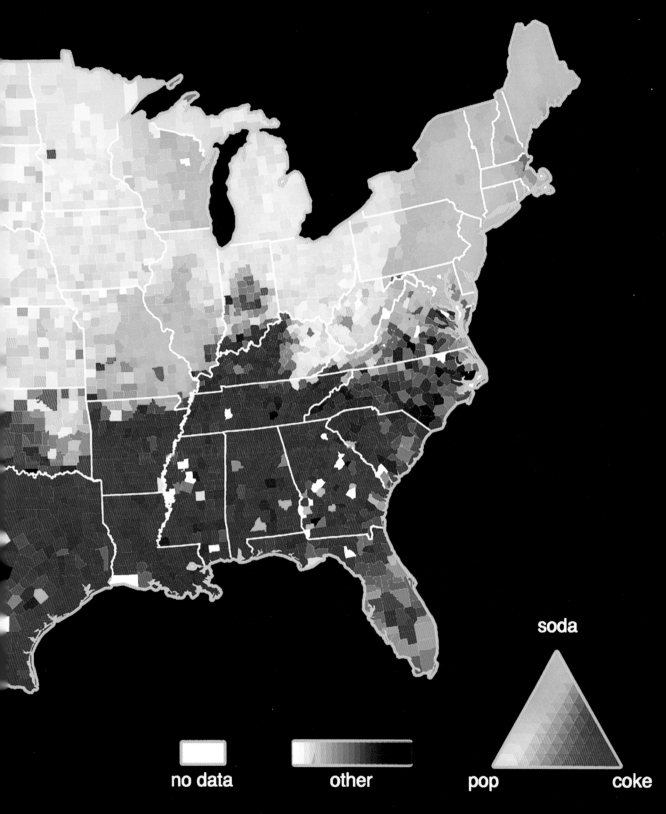

soda

no data   other   pop   coke

POP Quiz

1. WHAT BRAND OF TRUCK DID THE FEIGENSONS FIRST BUY?

A. Ford
B. Packard
C. GMC
D. Dodge

2. WHICH OF THESE POPS IS EVEN OLDER THAN FAYGO?

A. Pop Tarts
B. Pillsbury's Poppin' Fresh doughboy
C. Snap, Crackle, Pop
D. Pop Rocks candy
E. Popsicle

3. WHICH OF THESE WAS NOT A 1965 FAYGO DIET RECIPE?

A. Creamy asparagus cheese salad mold
B. Hawaiian ribs in root beer sauce
C. Faygo passion fruit punch borscht
D. Green beans au Faygo

4. WHICH IS NOT WELCOME AT A DETROIT LUNCH?

A. Coney dog with ketchup
B. Germack nuts
C. Better Made potato chips
D. A Sanders cream puff sundae

5. HOW MANY OTHER WORDS CAN BE SPELLED USING ALL THE LETTERS IN FAYGO?

A. Six
B. Four
C. Three
D. Two
E. None

6. WHICH IS NOT A TRUE FLAVOR IN THE OHANA LINE, INTRODUCED IN 1996?

A. Punch
B. Pineapple
C. Mango punch
D. Lemonade
E. Kiwi strawberry

The Elements

313 **190.7**

Fa

Faygo

The Feigensons sold soda water in pressurized siphons, or syphons. The lever would release the soda. Ice could make the bottles explode.

Fizzical Science

Pop is about 90 percent carbonated water, also called sparkling water, soda water, seltzer water, or just plain soda or seltzer. Club soda is a whole other thing. Most of the rest of pop is sweeteners, flavor, color, and preservatives. The carbonation is tiny bubbles of carbon dioxide injected into the water. Pressure holds them there. Without pressure, the bubbles rise out of the beverage and it goes flat. The effervescent bubbles tickle the tongue and can even make people sneeze.

As she wrote in this book's Foreword, Susie Feigenson remembers her father, Phil, would sometimes bring Faygo home for the family's table. She recalls stirring her Faygo with a spoon at one supper. Her father asked what she was doing. "I'm trying to get the bubbles out," she said. He convinced her he had been hard at work all day placing each bubble into the Faygo—with tweezers. She said she cried. "He was always a tease," she said. Harvey Lipsky, who joined Faygo as a chemist in the 1950s, speculated for a *Toledo Blade* reporter about how his children would celebrate Faygo's 100th anniversary in 2007. Lipsky said, "I think I'll get my kids together and maybe we'll have a pop can fight. [My grandsons] have a character named Faygo Man. They run around and Faygo Man fights Pepsi Man and beats him up, causing him to lose his bubbles." Getting the bubbles out of pop is child's play. The trick is putting them in there. To do that and to balance the bubbles with the other ingredients that make a pop that is fun and flavorful and feels right requires someone like Lipsky, a chemist. It's the science in the art of pop-making.

For thousands of years, people have bathed in naturally sparkling

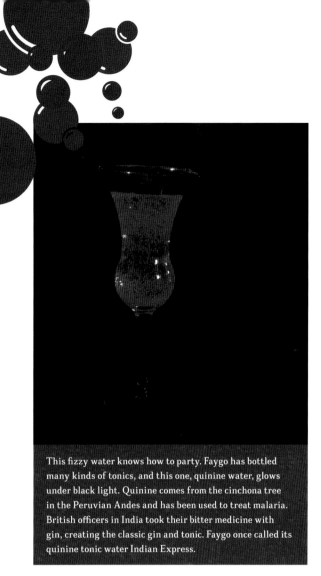

This fizzy water knows how to party. Faygo has bottled many kinds of tonics, and this one, quinine water, glows under black light. Quinine comes from the cinchona tree in the Peruvian Andes and has been used to treat malaria. British officers in India took their bitter medicine with gin, creating the classic gin and tonic. Faygo once called its quinine tonic water Indian Express.

Charles Alderton, another pharmacist, created Dr Pepper with a recipe of twenty-three ingredients in Waco, Texas, in 1885.

John Pemberton invented Coca-Cola in 1886 in Atlanta. He was also a pharmacist.

Pepsi-Cola, originally called Brad's Drink after inventor Caleb Bradham, was invented in New Bern, North Carolina, in 1893. Yes, Bradham was a pharmacist, too.

Pharmacists initially made their drinks for immediate consumption at a counter called a soda fountain. There was no "to go" about it and no need for bottles. Soda jerks moved us from liquid remedies to liquid refreshment. Soda jerks were typically young men in paper hats who mixed drinks at soda machines. Their name comes from the way they jerked their arms to shoot soda water into the glass.

To last beyond the soda fountain, however, carbonated drinks needed to be bottled under pressure. Pressurization injected a level of danger. One bottler advised:

> The large number of accidents that are constantly occurring from bursting syphons is due more to ignorance than carelessness of handling. Manufacturers should warn the customers that during sudden changes of temperature, syphons containing mineral water become dangerous. The rapid rise of the thermometer will sometimes increase the pressure 100 percent and produce violent explosions. Placing a syphon into a vessel containing ice will almost invariably shatter the bottle into fragments, causing serious injury.

mineral water for relaxation and health. In the late 1700s, they began drinking the water for its perceived medicinal properties. The first US patent for making mineral water was issued in 1809. It was made with sodium bicarbonate and acid, and was called "soda water." Soda water is kept pressurized in a siphon or syphon, also called a seltzer bottle, and released through a valve on the top of the container. Pharmacists began dispensing soda water by the glass, and then mixing it with tonics and remedies, also for medicinal reasons. Then they tried flavors.

Detroit pharmacist James Vernor came up with a ginger ale in 1866, the city's first soda pop.

Soda jerks made concoctions including flavored soda water, phosphates, lime rickeys, malts, and egg creams (which do not contain eggs). *World Telegram* photographer Alan Fisher caught this ice cream soda in 1936.

Photo courtesy of the Library of Congress

Bottle with Ease, Comfort and Safety

Stop Accidents!   Save Humanity!

USE
Krifka Bottlers' Protectors

Made to protect the arm, hand and face against flying glass from bursting bottles at all Filling Machines.

SOFT, PLIABLE, COMFORTABLE.

Glass cannot penetrate the arms, hands or face with Krifka Protectors.

Write us now

Krifka Bottlers' Protector Company
1750-52 W. Madison St.   CHICAGO, ILL.

A graphic public service announcement from the Krifka Bottlers' Protector Company from the 1921 *American Bottler*.

A worker mixes pop flavors at a line of shining Faygo vats in 1969. Only a few trusted employees knew the recipes, which were coded and locked up. *Photo credit: Howard Shirkey for the Detroit News. Walter P. Reuther Archives Library, Archives of Labor and Urban Affairs, Wayne State University*

The water has to be extremely pure because even invisible, harmless particles can kill carbonation, decreasing pop's shelf life and shipping range. Faygo worked hard to purify the water and hired chemists, bacteriologists, biologists, and other technical people, while few other bottlers did. Because Perry and Ben Feigenson began as bakers, not pharmacists, they never ran a soda fountain and they never thought they were selling medicine. Soon after they started their company, they dropped plans for beer and concentrated on flavoring seltzer with fruit. Matt Rosenthal, a grandson of Ben Feigenson who became Faygo's marketing director, told the *Toledo Blade* in 2007, "We always recognized the product for what it was. This is not penicillin. This is not a miracle drug of any sort. It's just pop."

Chief chemist Harvey Lipsky flaps a towel as Perry Feigenson did when he mixed Faygo's mysteriolicious Rock & Rye. Lipsky found that without the towel and incantation, the pop wouldn't come out right. *Photo credit: Howard Shirkey for the* Detroit News. *Walter P. Reuther Archives Library, Archives of Labor and Urban Affairs, Wayne State University*

Flavor Purveyors

The ingredient that makes pop distinctive is flavoring, of course. Although the industry became dominated by one-flavor powerhouses such as Coca-Cola and 7UP, Faygo was one of many companies to offer what it called "a rainbow of flavors." According to a 1998 Faygo press release, company president Stan Sheridan said, "Our business is flavors and our customers anxiously expect new flavors and products. We've been giving them unique variety for 90 years." This makes sense for a company founded by bakers. Just imagine a cake shop that has only one kind of frosting. Faygo pops have included some hits, some flops, and one flavor that literally exploded.

In 1972, Mort Feigenson told *Detroit News* writer Tish Myers, "It takes 107 ingredients to produce our current line of 28 flavors." Fruit

flavors contained pure squeezings reduced to concentrated bases. Mort said, "It takes about 45 pounds of raw fruit to equal one gallon of extract. We take what nature has given us and enhance upon it." When Faygo senior flavorist Hoyt McIntosh was interviewed in 1995 by *Detroit Free Press* writer Patty LaNoue Stearns, Faygo was in thirty-three states and had forty-three flavors. McIntosh was a twenty-six-year employee who had worked his way up from quality control technician to flavorist. He had degrees in engineering and mathematics. He said that he and his predecessor, John L. Laughlin Jr., as well as the flavorists before them, guarded Faygo's formulae like treasures. In the 1960s, a tester had such pitch-perfect taste buds that his (or her) identity was kept under wraps and they were not told how influential their advice was. One of the top secrets was how to make Rock & Rye. Even late into his career, founder Perry Feigenson mixed that one. In a 1969 *Detroit News Magazine* article Lipsky recalled, "One day when he was in his 80s and having a tough time climbing the stairs to the lab, he called me aside and said he figured it was time to learn the secret. I watched the mumbo-jumbo, which included waving a towel over the bottle, and I took notes. I analyzed the process and, being a chemist, figured I could duplicate the blend by modern methods. I worked on it several months, using the latest scientific steps. It smelled the same, it looked the same, but it wasn't the same. I now make it his way—even waving a towel over the bottle. I never have figured out what that did to the blend."

Faygo did not invent Rock & Rye. Wegener's of Detroit made a Rock & Rye in 1885. The company was established in 1870 and called itself Detroit's first soft-drink manufacturer, though Vernors was invented in 1866. Rock & Rye was modeled after America's first bottled cocktail. Rye whiskey, being harsher than whiskeys made primarily from barley and corn, was sometimes smoothed out with crystalized sugar, called rock candy. That's where the name Rock & Rye comes from. The drink was flavored with orange and lemon, as well as bitters or spices, such as cinnamon and horehound. Some teetotalers drank Rock & Rye for its "medicinal properties."

In the 1880s, Nathan Van Beil of New York City marketed a tonic called "Rye and Rock," which he declared "has proved immense success in the cure of lung, throat, malarial and vocal diseases." He advertised that "Signor Campinini, the world-renowned tenor, says: 'Van Beil's Rye and Rock is an inestimable friend to my throat as it instantaneously relieves hoarseness.'" Van Beil declared on the bottle, "My trademark consists of the words 'Rye and Rock'; any change on these words is an infringement. The law recognizes no claims of ignorance of the statutes. Dealers in imitation or counterfeit goods will be prosecuted." Van Beil sued other bottlers, including Wegener's, but never won, and the company disappeared around 1900. Bottled Rock & Rye cocktails are still sold, but they do not taste at all like the pop.

When people yearned for pre-Prohibition times, they reminisced with a song about a hobo's paradise, "Big Rock Candy Mountain." When its

USE VAN BEIL'S RYE AND ROCK

THE TONIC
AND ONLY CURE
FOR COUGHS, COLDS AND CONSUMPTION·

This 1888 ad targeted Victorian women who wouldn't dare drink, but who needed their medicine. An 1880 ditty went, "He's rock and rye crazy, down in the dock, you'll see by his nose he loves rye and rock." *Photo courtesy of the Library of Congress*

Popular Prohibition-era products included non-alcoholic substitutes Rock & Rye, lime rickey, root beer, ginger ale, and mixers to smooth out nasty homemade alcohol. Rock & Rye's flavor is hard to pin down. Faygo calls it a cream cola.

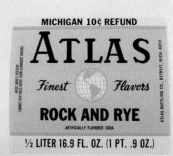

Atlas was one of several Detroit bottlers that made Rock & Rye pop. The Tomaszewski family owned the factory on the Detroit-Hamtramck border. Detroit's original Rock & Rye was likely made by Wegener's, established in 1870.

lyrics were sanitized to turn it into a kids' song, "rock and rye springs" became "lemonade springs," "cigarette trees" became "lollipop trees," and "little streams of alkyhol" became "streams of soda pop." During Prohibition, Faygo saw root beer sales climb and came out with its Rock & Rye. Wegener's advertised its Rock & Rye as "a blended mixing drink." Mort Feigenson said the company also sold ginger ale to speakeasies that mixed it with rotgut. After Prohibition, Faygo obtained a permit to brew beer but gave up on it to concentrate on its core business. Pretend-beer Faygo Bräu and faux-wine Chateaux Faygeaux came decades after Prohibition.

McIntosh said, "It goes back to the original Feigensons—they demanded a certain mystique and secrecy. There are very few people who actually know the true identities of the materials." Recipes were coded, and most staffers handling pop potions had been with Faygo for at least

Serious Eats rated Faygo's grape pop as the fourth-best in the country. The review said, "Some praised it for its intense sweetness, while others docked points for the very same reason."

twenty years. McIntosh's predecessor had retired from Foote & Jenks Corp., a flavor company in Jackson, Michigan, in 1971, and joined Faygo to help with the diet flavors. Foote & Jenks had been founded in a pharmacy in 1884. It made flavorings and fragrances from oils, roots, and spices. Its lemon flavoring was so powerful that one gallon could make thirty thousand bottles of pop. Its products were used in other companies' drinks, food, medicines, and perfumes.

When Zlati Meyer, an Orthodox Jewish reporter who grew up with New York soda, moved to Detroit to work for the *Free Press*, she was delighted to find that all Faygo flavors were kosher, even the grape. Under the strictest kashrut, or Jewish dietary laws, grape juice must be handled differently than the juice of other fruits. That is because of the chance, however slight, that the juice might turn into wine. Grape juice must be "cooked" under supervision before it can be handled by non-Jews. Irving Sarnoff explained the Passover certification process for the *Free Press* in 1975. He said he was one of fifteen "mashgichim," or supervisors, contracted out by the Council of Orthodox Rabbis of Greater Detroit to hospitals, caterers, and nursing homes. You might notice that some product lines, such as Slurpee, specify that all their flavors are kosher except the grape. For Passover, Faygo had to certify that the ingredients and equipment had not been in contact with any leaven, or hametz, which is off-limits during the eight days of Passover. Most kosher-observant American Jews also avoid products made with corn, including corn sweeteners. For Faygo to be

This is how *Bon Appétit* described Faygo root beer, which it ranked the number-one root beer in the land in 2009: "Dry and crisp, with a frothy head, a good bite, and a long finish."

In a 2011 national taste test, Serious Eats named Faygo orange as its winner.

acceptable during Passover, equipment had to remain idle for twenty-four hours. Then the lines cranked up and produced 1.73 million bottles of kosher-for-Passover Faygo sweetened with cane sugar.

Translating frosting flavors into pop was outstanding alchemy, Faygo's Lipsky said in a Channel 7 interview for the company's centennial. "I was here for eleven years before they told me how to do it, and I'm a chemist and I couldn't believe it could be done. . . . My claim to fame was after we did some technical work to extend the shelf life of those cake flavors; I basically had nothing to do. So, they turned me loose on new flavors and gave

me the formulas. . . . We haven't decided what new flavor our centennial flavor is, but we have decided to begin a contest and let the public name and kind of create the flavor for us, and the winner will get his picture on the label." Faygo's centennial flavor wound up as a blueberry-vanilla combination.

Lipsky started with the company when it was forty-eight years old and became vice president of research and development. He told the *Free Press* in 1995 that flavor testing was not a formal process. Lipsky said he, Sheridan, Rosenthal, and a few other key staffers would take a sip and then grin or grimace. Susie Feigenson, Phil's eldest daughter, had early experience with flavors, as she wrote in the Foreword. She said her father worked all around the factory. He visited the loading dock, lines for washing and filling bottles, and, most importantly to her, the syrup room. She recalls this ritual: "When he would come home, I'd hug him and put my nose against his shirt and smell what flavor he had been mixing that day. Some days he would be orange, some days grape, some days strawberry. He'd be root beer some days." She recalls testing samples when she worked at Faygo in 1967. Someone came around with little cups of the new brew, and employees were asked to try a sip. They signified their opinion by marking a big-smile smiley face, a moderate-smile smiley face, a neutral face with a straight line for a mouth, or a frown.

Rosenthal told the *Free Press*, "We have people here who just know when it's right. . . . Everybody tastes it and comments on it, Harvey takes a look at the comments and makes adjustments if necessary. But it doesn't take very long. Hoyt can change the formula five times in one day—it works that quickly if we have to." Rosenthal said prospective flavors were also tested by Faygo's law firm or ad agency or the marketing class at nearby Martin Luther King Jr. High School. Lipsky said a new flavor could be in stores within weeks because Faygo employed on-site chemists and taste technicians. In 1992, *Crain's Detroit Business* reported that launching a flavor cost Faygo about fifty thousand dollars and that four new ones might come out each year.

The spectrum of flavors and companies, even early in the nineteenth century, is evident in the 1912 report of the Michigan Dairy and Food Commission's pop inspections. It tested drinks from bottlers in three dozen Michigan cities. Its list of violators had more than 400 pops including:

Banana pop
Black pop
Blood orange pop
Chocolate cream
Cocola
Cola koke
Cremo ginger
Cuban ade
Dreamo
Gin seng
Grapemist
Iron port
Kolatona
Kos-Kola-Pop
Lemon pop
Orange cider
Orange pop
Orcharade
Peach mellow
Ple Zee
Rasport
Raspberry wine
Red pop
Red tame cherry
Sherbet
Strawberry pop
White pop

For a pop to succeed, the timing has to be as precise as the flavor. When Faygo released a cotton candy flavor on live TV on May 9, 2014, Al Chittaro, then executive vice president, said, "We've had the flavor in our arsenal for probably five years and were just waiting for the right time to introduce it to the market. This happens to be our fifty-fourth flavor." A 2011 announcement had quoted Chittaro as saying, "Our summer lineup of new flavors brings Faygo's total to fifty-six different sodas and noncarbonated beverages and truly means Faygo has something for every taste." Besides adding flavors, Faygo also retired them. Arctic Sun was developed as a wine-cooler alternative and not released for eight years. When coolers started losing steam, Faygo removed Arctic Sun's cloudy wine-color look and brought it out as a clear pop in the 1990s. Initially, sales were good. When they flagged, Arctic Sun was retired. In a May 19, 2017, Facebook Live event shot in the company's vault, Arctic Sun was rereleased for Faygo's 110th year.

Some of Lipsky's favorite Faygo flops were the early lithiated lemon, ginger beer with lithium salts; apple-flavored Eve; Dr Mort (flavored like Dr Pepper and later rebranded as Dr Faygo); India Express tonic water; vanilla pop; gold port; the non-alcoholic wine-like Chateaux Faygeaux; early diet flavor redpopcola, and Old California lime.

And this leads to the story of the exploding Royal Hawaiian pineapple-orange. As Lipsky told *Free Press* reporter Stearns, the new pop was introduced at the Pick-Fort Shelby Hotel: "It was 1961 or '62. . . . Everyone's wearing a Hawaiian shirt, we have pineapples on every table, every wife got to

An early Faygo lemon contained lithium salt, a mood stabilizer. This cap shows an early Faygo logo.

take a pineapple home." The bottles went to stores on Monday, and, buoyed by Faygo's reputation and a marketing campaign, it launched well. A week later, the pineapple juice, which had not been sterilized, began turning rancid. Pressure built up, and the bottles starting blowing their tops. Caps were hitting ceilings in the Faygo warehouse and breaking light bulbs. They were doing similar things inside stores.

The *Free Press* article said Lipsky cringed: "Oh, was it dead. And the complications it caused— the mayor of Dearborn called, wanted it out of Dearborn by such and such a date. Our drivers went out and picked up all the products. A week after that, the drivers wouldn't come to work, then declared a one-day strike."

Once Dole supplied sterilized juice, the pop stopped popping, and pineapple-orange became a successful, if quieter, flavor.

Whether hits, flops, or explosive, the all-time number of Faygo pops is hard to pin down because the lineup is always changing. The strategy was to sell a lot of different flavors rather than bank on just one or two. Mort wrote in 1967, "Our future development strategy is taking into account that the average consumer may eventually become as fickle about types of soft drinks as about types of automobiles. We plan to always have five or six unique products in our line, each of which can be depended upon to generate two or three years of volume sales before requiring replacement by some newer and different taste appeal. We've always been an oddball." The company wanted to "blanket the specialty drink segment rather than rely on one particular drink." He said that strawberry was most popular: "Ten years ago, we started calling it redpop, and everyone laughed. Anyone who even suggested a name like that at Coca-Cola would have been fired on the spot. For us, it sells." Chittaro attributed Faygo's success to "the unique flavors we come up with every year—two or three every year. And when they slow down, we get rid of the old ones and we have the mainstay flavors so we can continue to evolve and continue to come up with fun, new flavors every year."

A list of Faygo flavors, which has to be considered partial, is in the back of this book.

Oh, Sugar!

If most of pop is carbonated water and if flavoring gives it its character, the controversy is in the sweeteners. Price, availability, wartime rationing, waistlines, and health have shaped the industry.

There are many natural sweeteners. We find sugar in cane, beets, corn syrup, sorghum syrup, maple syrup, agave and other nectars, fruits, and honey. Some sugars work better in pop than others. The best sweetener has good taste and mouthfeel and combines well with the other ingredients. Cane sugar works very well in pop, but natural sugars are almost always more costly and caloric than artificial sweeteners.

Artificial sweetening has been around for a long time, and by the time the Feigensons started making pop in 1907, saccharin, made from coal tar derivatives, was widely used in drinks and canned goods. Most major artificial sweeteners (saccharin, cyclamates, aspartame, and sucralose) were discovered when scientists were on break, licked their fingers, and—eureka!

In 1908, the US Department of Agriculture's chief chemist and the father of the Food and Drug Administration, Harvey Wiley, recommended that the nonnutritive sweetener saccharin be classified as a toxin and banned. He ran into two opposing forces: President Teddy Roosevelt's waistline and World War I.

1911 Sampson trucks owned by Edgar's Sugar House showed its prosperity. The H. Edgar & Son warehouse at Lafayette Boulevard and Twelfth by the railroad tracks supplied sugar to many Detroit companies. Detroit's 1914 City Directory listed C. Goodloe Edgar as president and Mary Edgar as secretary. *Photo courtesy of the National Automotive History Collection, Detroit Public Library*

Roosevelt, whose diet substituted saccharin for sugar, explained: "Anybody who says saccharin is injurious to health is an idiot." In 1910, Roosevelt appointed a Referee Board of Consulting Scientific Experts. Its first mission was to study the effect of the additives sodium benzoate and saccharin on people's health. Dr. Ira Remsen, the Johns Hopkins professor who had discovered saccharin by licking his fingers, was asked to chair the board. Remsen and the board confirmed Roosevelt's judgment about Wiley and concluded that saccharin was perfectly fine in small doses. The United States became so involved in sugar issues that sometimes it toppled governments over it.

In November and December of 1912, before saccharin was cleared, Michigan's Dairy and Food Commission inspectors scoured the state for soft drinks containing it. Of the 731 samples they tested, 447 were listed as misbranded or adulterated. This usually meant they contained saccharin. The commission had almost sixty-nine thousand bottles of pop destroyed. Feigenson drinks were not cited.

While the Feigensons avoided Michigan's 1912 saccharin purge, they were in court in 1915 in what the *Detroit Free Press* called "probably the first local dispute precipitated by the European war." It was about the price of sugar and involved a

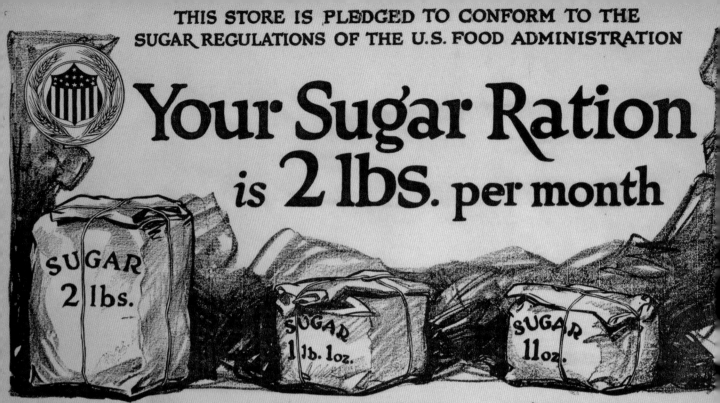

THIS STORE IS PLEDGED TO CONFORM TO THE
SUGAR REGULATIONS OF THE U.S. FOOD ADMINISTRATION

Your Sugar Ration
is 2 lbs. per month

SUGAR
2 lbs.

SUGAR
1 lb. 1 oz.

SUGAR
11 oz.

AMERICA'S VOLUNTARY RATION
ENGLAND'S COMPULSORY RATION

FRANCE'S COMPULSORY RATION

ITALY'S COMPULSORY RATION

We must confine our consumption of Sugar to not more than 2 lbs. per person per month in order to provide a restricted ration to England, France and Italy.

A comparison showed how much tighter supplies were for allies in France and Italy. The US Food Administration's recommended limit of two pounds of sugar per person per month in 1917 was the law in England. *Image courtesy of the Library of Congress, US Food Administration*

major Detroit sugar supplier. Known informally as Edgar's Sugar House, H. Edgar & Son dated back to the 1860s. Edgar was a chief sugar supplier to Faygo and many Detroit pop bottlers and bakers. In 1875, Edgar & Son had loaned Fred Sanders a barrel of sugar, which he used to start an iconic Detroit candy company in his name.

The Feigensons said that H. Edgar & Son had agreed in 1914 to sell them sugar at $1.65 a sack. They left a thousand-dollar check, took a hundred sacks, and said they would come back for two hundred more later. Soon after war began in Europe, sugar prices jumped to eight dollars a sack. H. Edgar & Son said it had told the Feigensons to take the sugar when they had the chance and that they would not honor the prewar price. The Feigensons dropped the matter.

After the United States entered the war in 1917, Roosevelt's wise tolerance of saccharin was affirmed, as the country needed to redeploy

Sugar means Ships

The sugar used in sweet drinks must be brought to America in ships. Last year 400,000,000 lbs of sugar were imported for sweet drinks. These ships must now be used to carry soldiers to the front

Drink less sweetened beverages

We are at war

ICE CREAM AND ICE COLD SODA

Every Spoonful — Every Sip — Means less for a Fighter

U. S. Food Administration.

"Drink less sweetened beverages. We are at war," took direct aim at pop. Notice the soda jerk inside. Faygo was sold by the bottle during World War I, not in soda shops. *Image courtesy of the Library of Congress, US Food Administration*

UNCLE SAM

THE LID'S DOWN!

FAMILY SUGAR BOWL

OBEY ORDERS! U. S. Food Administration

Uncle Sam's wishes were clear during The Great War, but mandatory rationing did not come until World War II. *Image courtesy of the Library of Congress, US Food Administration*

Sugar means Ships

The Consumption of Sugar Sweetened Drinks Must be Reduced.

For your beverages 400 million lbs. of sugar were imported in *Ships* last year. Every *Ship* is needed to carry soldiers and supplies *now*.

This poster shows how ships for the transport of vital wartime soldiers, arms, supplies, and food were being diverted to carry sugar to a woman sucking it up through a soda glass. On the European shore, a soldier beckons "Hurry." *Image courtesy of the Library of Congress, US Food Administration*

ships from moving mountains of sugar to moving men and matériel. To keep sugar affordable and prevent hoarding, some countries rationed quantities, and saccharin was in demand. The US Food Administration used voluntary rationing to persuade Americans to support the war effort. It plastered posters urging citizens to reduce consumption of meat, wheat, fats, and sugar throughout communities. President Woodrow Wilson appointed future president Herbert Hoover to direct the Food Administration. A 1918 Coca-Cola ad showed a hand holding up a glass of the beverage matching the silhouette of the Statue of Liberty's hand, holding up a torch. The ad said, "Your glass of Coca-Cola represents material allotted and authorized by Mr. Hoover and your Government after conservation has taken its heavy toll."

With the war over and Prohibition on in 1924, Perry was in court again over sugar, a key ingredient in alcohol. It seems 350 sacks of sugar had been stolen from an interstate shipment on the Michigan Central Railroad. The chief of the railway detectives' investigation led him to some men who were unloading freight. They directed him to a cartage company where a driver said he had hauled a truckload of sugar to the Feigenson bottling works.

Feigenson said he had no idea that the sugar, by then upstairs, was stolen. Two men who admitted stealing the sugar incriminated Feigenson to get lighter sentences. After the jury went into deliberations, the go-between who had arranged the sale told the judge Feigenson did not know

the sugar was stolen. When the jury announced a guilty verdict, the judge declared it to be the most extraordinary verdict he had ever heard. He said he had no choice but to sentence Feigenson to a five-thousand-dollar fine and one day in jail. Feigenson appealed and was exonerated. The

The federal government gave homemakers instructions, recipes, and substitutions for conserving sugar and other commodities needed overseas in World War I. *Image courtesy of the Library of Congress, US Food Administration*

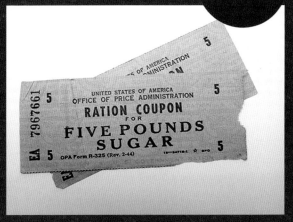

Detroiters line up for coupons in the spring of 1942, shortly after sugar rationing began. Sugar was the first commodity the United States rationed during World War II and the last one to be derationed. Limits stayed in place until 1947, well after the war ended.

Photo courtesy of the Library of Congress

sugar rustlers were sentenced to a year and a day in the federal pen in Atlanta. Justice can be sweet.

World War II brought mandatory rationing in 1942 and, on May 5, 1942, not five months after Pearl Harbor, the United States began rationing sugar, the first of all commodities to be restricted. The Office of Price Administration issued books of ration coupons. Faygo, other pop makers, candy makers, and bakers were cut to 80 percent of prewar supplies, then 50 percent. Manufacturers tried other sweeteners and recipes that required less sugar.

While most pop makers and confectioners suffered under rationing, one soft-drink maker prospered under it. Coca-Cola said it would make Coke available to all US military personnel in the world for a nickel a bottle, no matter what it cost the company. Coca-Cola issued a report on the importance of restful time for soldiers and workers. It played up the importance of refreshment, which happened to be one of its catchwords. A Coca-Cola executive was appointed to the sugar rationing board. Coke became a beverage of military necessity. The company faced no sugar restrictions when it made Coke for the military and its suppliers. In 1943, General George C. Marshall cabled Coca-Cola requisitioning equipment to build ten bottling plants, to supply three million bottles of Coke, and to provide enough materials to produce that much twice a month. While other pop makers struggled in the war, Coca-Cola found dominance.

Cyclamate's artificial sweetening properties had been discovered in 1937 by a graduate student who took a cigarette break without washing his hands and tasted sweetness on his fingers. Cyclamates came to market in the late 1950s and early 1960s. Wartime rationing had long since ended, but America's waistline was beginning to look like Teddy Roosevelt's. Lipsky said, "Then, as now, I was watching my weight . . . so I came up with the idea of what if these cake flavors were blended into diet soft drinks, and it worked and worked beautifully." Several pop makers came out with dietetic drinks in the 1960s, and that

Private Norman A. Martin of Detroit (right foreground) and other members of the Army National Guard's 133rd Field Artillery Battalion refresh with their first Coke in more than a year on March 2, 1944. They were dug in on the front lines near San Michele, Italy. Passing Cokes down to the gun position are Private John L. Hill of Louisville, Kentucky, and Private First Class Roy F. Jones of Marshall, Texas. *Photo courtesy of the Dwight D. Eisenhower Library*

was when Faygo introduced its line of artificially sweetened diet flavors.

For its sixtieth year, Faygo published a free recipe book called *One-Calorie Cookery* with recipes prepared by Weight Watchers. An ad for the 1967 book that was shaped like a bottle of Faygo said, "Diets don't have to be dull anymore. Here are fifteen fabulous recipes you can cook up with Faygo one-calorie flavors. Each recipe has been prepared by Weight Watchers of Eastern Michigan, an organization dedicated to turning the human body to ideal dimensions and physical condition." At the time, Detroiter Florine Mark had recently taken Weight Watchers classes in Queens, New York, where the organization was founded in 1963. Mark brought the franchise to

Michigan in 1966 and became the largest franchisee of Weight Watchers International.

By 1969, Americans were consuming seventeen million pounds of cyclamates, which are thirty to fifty times sweeter than sugar, per year. That October, cyclamates were found to cause cancer in rats, and the Food and Drug Administration, the group Roosevelt had fought over saccharin, banned cyclamates immediately. One headline said this would cause panic among beverage makers. Lipsky did not seem to be troubled. He told the *Detroit Free Press* that Faygo would have a new pop sweetened with sugar and saccharin within a week. Lipsky said, "It'll mean about two or three more calories an ounce, but that'll also mean a sweeter taste which could make the market for diet colas go even bigger than ever."

Mort Feigenson reported in the November 1969 issue of the *Food Dealer* that "because our laboratories are housed in the same building as our production operations, Faygo last month was able to start occupying empty supermarket soft drink department shelves with new low-calorie offerings within less than ten days following the cyclamate ban. First to reach retail levels was redpopcola, a newly formulated drink. And, second was a reformulated Faygo low-cal strawberry-cherry. Hopefully, Faygo's whole new lineup of eleven different low-calorie flavors will be in mass production and distribution by Thanksgiving Day." Because new federal regulations also allowed bottlers to mix artificial sweeteners with sugars, Mort predicted a rise of sales in better-tasting

low-calorie drinks. Some Faygo one-calorie pop cans later said they contained a saccharin blend.

The sweetness of sucralose, sold as Splenda, was discovered in 1976 when a lab assistant misunderstood "test" as "taste" and tasted the product. It has been used in hundreds of food products in the United States since 1999. One of sucralose's advantages over aspartame is that it stands up better to moderate baking temperatures.

The next ingredient to fall under health regulators' microscopes was the one that had put Teddy Roosevelt on a diet: real sugar. Worries intensified in 2009, when the *New England Journal of Medicine* reported that sweetened beverages, including those with high-fructose corn syrup, were the largest dietary contributor to obesity. The article proposed higher taxes to reduce consumption. Coca-Cola president Muhtar Kent responded in a *Wall Street Journal* op-ed with the headline "Coke Didn't Make America Fat." Kent wrote, in part, that the focus should be on how many calories we burn rather than on how many we consume. Dozens of cities voted on soft-drink taxes and several adopted them.

In New York City, Mayor Michael Bloomberg made sweet drinks a cause. He proposed a state tax but lost in the state legislature. He called for a ban on using food stamps for the drinks, but was turned back at the federal level. Next, he went after over-sized sugared drinks. Some drink cups hold more than a six-pack of cans, which is over half a gallon.

Cans became canvases when Faygo came out with this internationally themed diet series in 1977.

Bloomberg was scoffed at as "Nanny Bloomberg" for trying to regulate personal freedom. He used his influence and money to spread the cause. He poured twenty million dollars into successful campaigns for pop taxes in Philadelphia, San Francisco, and Oakland, California. Despite campaigns against sugar, Faygo and other beverage makers are offering real sugar as an alternative to high-fructose corn syrup.

Cook County, Illinois, home to Chicago, passed a controversial penny-per-ounce tax on sugary drinks, five times the amount charged on beer. Retailers, the Can the Tax Coalition, and so-called "Big Soda" were on one side of the issue. Health officials, people trying to close a county budget shortfall, and Bloomberg were among those on the other. The tax took effect July 1, 2017. It proved to be so unpopular and fell so short of revenue expectations that the board repealed it that October. The week before, legislators in Faygo's home state of Michigan had voted to ban local governments from imposing taxes on pop, even though none had tried. Some speculated that the Cook County reversal would kill the anti-pop movement.

We'll see.

POP Quiz

1. WHICH OF THESE WAS NOT A FAYGO FLAVOR?

A. Bright
B. Tango
C. Go
D. Sensation
E. 60/40

2. WHEN FAYGO LAUNCHED GOLD GINGER ALE, IT GAVE AWAY:

A. A bar of gold
B. A golden Cadillac
C. A gold-plated Faygo bottle
D. A year's supply of pop

3. FAYGO'S 60/40 IS 60 PERCENT GRAPEFRUIT. WHAT IS THE OTHER 40 PERCENT?

A. Cherry
B. Lime
C. Pineapple
D. Ginger

4. FAYGO HAD SEVERAL PIE-POPS. WHICH OF THESE IS THE FAKE?

A. Chocolate creme pie
B. Coconut cream pie
C. Key lime pie
D. Rhubarb pie
E. Cherry pie

5. IN A 1984 NEWSLETTER, FAYGO ASKED EMPLOYEES TO IDENTIFY ITS TOP 10 FLAVORS. WHICH OF THESE DID NOT MAKE THE LIST?

A. Redpop
B. Root beer
C. Rock & Rye
D. Grape
E. Punch

6. WHICH FLAVOR NEVER EXISTED?

A. Moon Mist green
B. Moon Mist red
C. Moon Mist blue
D. Moon Mist orange

The
Sons
Rise

Pivot Point

In February 1947, Faygo celebrated forty years in business with an awards banquet for employees. There, the torch was passed to the next generation of Feigensons, three World War II veterans who had joined the company the year before. Many family businesses fail to survive the first generation. Sometimes, there are no interested successors. And sometimes, the second generation has neither the skills nor the vision to take the helm or steer the enterprise to the next level. However, the Feigensons were deep in talent and interest. Perry's sons Morton and Herman, and Ben's only son, Philip, were ready.

The next fourteen months were somber ones, with Faygo offices closing twice for bereavement days. In November 1947, Mort and Herman's youngest brother, Albert, died at age 28. As a promising seventeen-year-old at Wayne State University,

Albert scored the highest in Detroit and in the top three nationally on an American Council of Education test. The following April, Faygo closed again for the funeral of co-founder Ben, 64. Perry kept working for at least ten more years, coming into the Gratiot Avenue office from nine a.m. to two p.m. In interviews with Chapman and the *Detroit Free Press*, Perry reflected on Faygo's past and shared his vision for its future. Perry, then age 77, said there were no plans to expand beyond Faygo's territory in southern Michigan. "Our job is to increase our share of the soft drink business in the area we already serve," he said. "There is enough business for us in Michigan, so why should we compete with our friends?" He had friends in Toledo, and his sisters-in-law had built Miller-Becker into Cleveland's largest independent soft-drink bottler, the Chapman report said. It said Feigenson protested when someone mentioned expanding Faygo's marketing area, recalling the days when cutthroat competition put many bottlers out of business. Perry lived until January 1964, when he was 81. Then, the new generation began tearing up the old script. Phil and Mort wanted Faygo to grow—by a lot.

The Chapman report described the successors' roles this way: "Mort Feigenson is vice president and oversees most of the advertising, sales and promotional activities of the company. His cousin, Phil, also is a vice president and directs production. Mort's brother Herman is the administrative man. He holds the title of secretary-treasurer and runs the business affairs inside the office." In

Using plastic cocktail stirrers, Perry Feigenson notes Faygo's fortieth birthday with his sons Morton, on his right, and Herman, on his left, and nephew Philip. Back from the war, they would take over leadership of the company.

Photo courtesy of the Feigenson family archives

Perry Feigenson, at 73, has climbed up into the cab of a steam shovel for the October 26, 1954, groundbreaking on a multimillion-dollar plant expansion. Perry came to work daily into the 1960s.

Photo courtesy of the Detroit Free Press

Cases and cases of lemon-lime Uptown up to ten layers high dwarf Perry and Phil in this sidewalk promotion. *Photo courtesy of the Feigenson family archives*

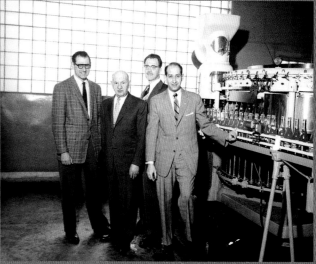

The Feigenson leadership inside the plant at 3579 Gratiot Avenue. *From left:* Mort, vice president; Perry, co-founder and president; Herman, secretary-treasurer, and Phil, vice president. *Photo courtesy of the Feigenson family archives*

1983, *Detroit Free Press* marketing writer Betsey Hansell described the cousins' roles in a profile about Mort. Hansell wrote about his passion for riding horses, which took his mind off business concerns. When he rode, "He isn't thinking about W. B. Doner & Co.'s storyboards for two new Faygo commercials . . . He isn't thinking about cousin Phil . . .who is in Los Angeles today scouting for a bottler to produce Faygo in California." Mort and Phil had emerged as the go-to guys. Susie characterized Mort as Faygo's front man and public voice, while her father worked behind the scenes. She said her dad frequently visited the flavor room, bottling line, truck bays, and other production areas. "In the winter," she said, "until he knew those trucks were back and everyone was safe, he wouldn't come home. If he did and then

there was a snowstorm, he would go back to the plant and check to see that everybody had come in. It was his baby and he had to put it to bed." Susie and newspaper accounts described Mort and Phil as sharing an office and sharing decisions. Hansell wrote that the two worked "side by side at two six-foot desks and a couple of tables all shoved together and flanked by six old-fashioned black telephones. Neither Feigenson has ever had a secretary." Susie recalls that there was no grandiose sign on the door and that her father had a simple nameplate on his desk. She keeps it in her home as a memento. Susie said the cousins were equal partners in everything. She said they often drove places together and were lunchtime regulars at Joe Muer's seafood restaurant south on Gratiot Avenue. One day, she said, as the cousins drove

Phil, right, and Mort in 1969 wear the paper hats the company sometimes called "Faygo caps." This was around the time Faygo's expansion to new markets fueled rumors that it would seek outside investors. *Photo credit: Howard Shirkey for the Detroit News. Walter P. Reuther Archives Library, Archives of Labor and Urban Affairs, Wayne State University*

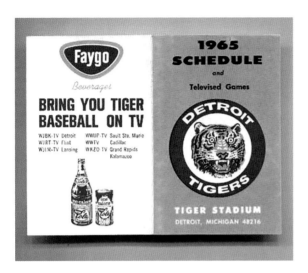

Faygo bolstered its 1965 Detroit Tigers TV advertising with pocket schedules. Several companies listed the games on small schedules and matchbooks.

Community, 1945–1995, the Tigers stopped selling slots to a few major sponsors, including Detroit brewers Goebel and Stroh, and opened slots to smaller advertisers who could afford just a few commercials. The man in charge of the change, "Doc" Fenkell, sold few spots in the first part of the season. He said he knew "nothing about television except how to turn it on."

Mort recalled for a *Forbes* interview in 1982 that Faygo agreed to buy a pair of sixty-second spots. Three weeks before the commercials were to run, advertising agency Doner called with bad news. Mort said, "They told me, much to my horror, that it was too expensive to black out northern Michigan and Toledo, so our commercials were going to play there at no extra cost." The problem? There was no Faygo in those places.

along Gratiot Avenue, her father spotted a twenty-dollar bill in the middle of the street. They stopped, collected the bill, and split it fifty-fifty.

Mort acquired the title of company president, and Phil reflected the Feigenson egalitarianism when he said that the cousins did not stand on titles: "All three of us are at various times bosses, and most of the time nothing more than employees." But the cousins did not want to follow Perry's prescription of being confined to the existing market. They wanted to go big. One of the first moves came in 1965, the year after Perry died. If you didn't know the Feigensons better, you'd think they bumbled into their big break. That year, the Detroit Tigers baseball team changed the way it sold local TV advertising. According to Patrick Joseph Harrigan's *The Detroit Tigers: Club and*

In 1965, when Faygo first advertised during televised Detroit Tigers games, Guy's Nut and Candy Company of Kansas City, Missouri, distributed this pin. It released them in 1962, 1965, and 1966. Years later, Guy's had snacks made in Detroit.

DETROIT WINS

WITH THE AID OF

TYRUS COBB

WHO ALWAYS DRINKS

Coca-Cola

Tyrus Cobb, who has been largely responsible for the wonderful showing of the Detroit Club in 1907, says:

"I drink Coca-Cola regularly throughout all seasons of the year. On days when we are playing a double-header I always find that a drink of Coca-Cola between the games refreshes me to such an extent that I can start the second game feeling as if I had not been exercising at all, in spite of my exertions in the first."

He has found that Coca-Cola is of real assistance to him in his batting, fielding and wonderful base-running — is invigorating and has no "let down" or harmful after effects.

YOU will like Coca-Cola — delicious, refreshing and invigorating.

5c everywhere.

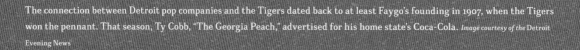

The connection between Detroit pop companies and the Tigers dated back to at least Faygo's founding in 1907, when the Tigers won the pennant. That season, Ty Cobb, "The Georgia Peach," advertised for his home state's Coca-Cola. *Image courtesy of the Detroit Evening News*

Faygo quickly scraped together thirty thousand dollars for food brokers who arranged to get Faygo into the grocery stores in time for the commercials. Viewers went for the Faygo. Seeing the success of the Tigers advertising, the Feigensons began thinking regionally. In January, two years after his father's death, Mort said Faygo would not rule out a national expansion. The expansion of Faygo's footprint from those 1965 Tigers game ads catalyzed changes in market area, production, bottling, and distribution, catapulting the company to a whole new level.

Free Press business writer Ken Thompson reported that by early 1966, "The Feigensons have followed a pattern only a private ownership could pursue—plowing a large part of earnings back into the business. In recent years, they've put $1 million into more mechanized equipment and improvements." He also reported that advertising, which cost Faygo more than $325,000 in 1965, would stay strong, although Tigers TV games would not be part of the plan. Thompson reported that, with pop by then a year-round beverage, Faygo had sold the equivalent of 18.3 million eight-ounce bottles in December, just shy of what the company had sold in June. Thompson declared that, despite Perry's hands-off philosophy, "Toledo, Fort Wayne and South Bend markets have already been successfully invaded."

In 1967, Faygo's sixtieth anniversary, Mort wrote about letters from Detroiters who had moved for jobs across the country, imploring Faygo to ship Redpop, Rock & Rye, root beer, and

Ads for Uptown, including an image of Herkimer Bottleneck, decorated the Feigensons' simple office when the *National Bottlers' Gazette* shot this photo of Mort.
Photo courtesy of the Feigenson family archives

other favorites to their new homes. Mort said this demand would be met "in the not too distant future" and repeated ambitions for national distribution. This would require many changes and, eventually, a structural change.

That year, Faygo surpassed Coca-Cola to become Detroit's number-two sales leader, after only Pepsi-Cola, in take-home sales. In a TV interview, Lipsky said: "I remember when I started here there were sixteen bottlers in this area and Faygo,

After hay-burning transportation was put out to pasture, Faygo invested heavily in trucks and gasoline. This was part of its fleet of fifty trucks, which featured a logo topped by lions on either side of a shield bearing the letter *F*. *Photo courtesy of the Feigenson family archives*

Coke, and Pepsi; there are only three now. So, we sort of figured out how to survive."

In July 1968, Mort reported that Faygo had met with more than fifty food buyers in Ohio and was expanding that market into Akron, Canton, Youngstown, Warren, and Cleveland, where Ben had initially worked for his wife's family. In September, Faygo crossed the Detroit River a few miles from the plant and began selling in Canada.

After Faygo began bottling near Toronto in April 1969 and sales increased, people speculated that family-run Faygo would become publicly owned. Mort stole the headlines at a September 16, 1969, Detroit Press Club luncheon recognizing advertising agency W. B. Doner. Mort said Faygo aspired to reach 70 percent of the US market by 1975. He said the company wanted to be in Pittsburgh in early 1970 and would then reach the plant's capacity. "At that point, we will have to make a decision about outside financing . . . capital has to come from somewhere." He said this would likely mean selling shares in the company. The change the Feigensons had ignited would go beyond that.

Innovation Station

Modernizing an aged plant into a regional or national operation required changes in the supply chain from labeling to bottling, packaging and distribution, and in advertising and product development. Integrating these upgraded processes would be as intricate as balancing the ingredients for a new flavor of pop.

At this time, Mort was writing a regular column in the Associated Food Dealers' publication. Innovation was his favorite subject, and he hit it on several fronts: low-calorie flavors, advertising, expansion, deliveries, and bottles. He advocated working SYNERGISTICALLY, a word he stressed with all caps, to keep Faygo alongside store brands, which he said helped everyone.

Part of what made this possible was a new delivery system. When Faygo was small and pop was perishable, "store-door" deliveries made sense. Faygo delivered bottles and cans directly to the point of sale in its own trucks. Now, the Feigensons signed deals to deliver semi-truck loads to warehouses,

Faygo briefly distributed Kayo, a chocolate soft drink invented in the 1920s in Chicago by another Russian immigrant, Aaron D. "Doc" Pashkow. The drink was named after Chicago comic strip character Kayo Mullins, and his mug advertised the drink. Kayo was the kid brother of the strip's star, fighter Moonshine "Moon" Mullins.

where chains put them on their own trucks with soup, cereal, and other food products. Mort quoted the general manager of one independent wholesaler, who said, "A good wholesaler can distribute soft drinks to his retailers at half the costs of the bottler's store-door methods." In June 1971, Mort credited warehouse distribution with Faygo's success in Pittsburgh. By November, he was

This tin portrait of Kayo Mullins was a prize in boxes of Cracker Jack popcorn and peanuts.

Faygo tried a number of marketing approaches with its cans and bottles. The faces collection did well in testing in 1977, but not as well in the market. Faygo did an about-face in 1979, returning to fruit.

profiling P & C Food Markets in Syracuse, whose warehouse was taking a million cases of Faygo a year and pioneering a measure of profitability per square foot of shelf space.

Faygo reconfigured its plant. In 1966, a $500,000 expansion split bottle and can operations, and warehouse space was added to increase production. In 1967, the company doubled its water-polishing capacity to 20,000 gallons an hour. A $100,000 investment bought Faygo an 84-spout bottle-filling machine, the fastest ever built. In April 1969, Mort announced Faygo had

spent $200,000 to speed up its quart-bottling operation from 200 bottles a minute to 250.

It introduced new flavors and new lines of beverages, including more low-calorie options, a caffeine-free Faygo cola in 1968, and a non-alcoholic Faygo Bräu that foamed like real beer. In November 1970, Mort noted, "Faygo's product development people average one success for about every ten failures. But their batting average is more than satisfactory when they hit on a unique soft drink concept like Faygo Bräu, our non-alcoholic ginger beer. Although introduced only five months

After Faygo Bräu's launch, Mort Feigenson said it was very popular with teen and younger consumers, whom the company hoped would enter a "long-lasting love affair with Faygo Bräu's taste and its head-foaming traits." However, the frothy bräu soon fizzled.

In 1984, Faygo packaged Mandarin orange pop in cans lettered in Arabic. Besides Mandarin orange, the cans say, "Sugar free, soft drink, sparkling water with added orange juice." Oh, and of course, the cans also say Faygo.

ago, Faygo Bräu is already our third-best-selling offering." *Free Press* reporter Thompson called Faygo's investment in developing nonreturnable bottles "huge." They pleased shoppers, sellers, and companies. A Faygo ad aimed at the *Food Dealer*'s audience of retailers asked, "Did we put Faygo in no-return bottles for you or your customers?" It answered, "Yes." Another ad promoted a pioneering Faygo twist cap that let people reseal bottles to preserve the bubbles.

In November 1971, Mort reported that after expanding its reach for six years, the out-of-state market was bringing Faygo 40 percent of its sales volume. Detroit-area sales were also growing. Faygo ordered twenty-five more forty-five-foot truck trailers to keep up. Mort called warehouse distribution "the most meaningful move we have made yet." And in January 1972, for its first national sales meeting, Faygo invited sales representatives and brokers in the United States and Canada as well as advertising agencies. The company was now hiring talent away from Chrysler Corp. and General Foods.

Bottlenecked

Historically, bottlers have had some devilish business models. Because glass bottles initially cost more than what went inside, bottlers had to get them back and reuse them over and over again or lose money on every sale. Bottlers who did not retrieve and reuse their bottles would go broke. A bottler's survival depended on how well it managed the bottle end of the business. The bottle was—all in one—container, point-of-purchase marketing message, and a significant share of a bottler's assets. It was the bottles, in fact, that gave Faygo its name. In 1920, deciding that Feigenson Brothers was too long or too expensive to put on bottles, the founders shortened the name to Faygo.

Issues with bottles bound beer and soda pop makers together. They conferenced and commiserated under the banner of the American Bottlers' Protective Association. The monthly publication, established in 1881, was the *American Carbonator and Bottler*, "Devoted to the general bottling trade and the soda water counter." Its name was later shortened to the *American Bottler*. At the American Bottlers' 1911 convention in Chicago, the Feigensons applied to join.

In bottling's early days, there were laws, fines, and jail terms for bottle rustlers who resold a bottler's empties to other companies. Bottles were embossed with the warning "This bottle

An early Feigenson "blob top" bottle. Molten glass was applied and tooled around the top of the bottle when it came out of the mold. The mold embossed the words, and a stopper plugged the bottle.

not to be sold," an admonition that bottles should be returned to the owner and not someone else. Miller-Becker in Cleveland, run by Feigenson in-laws, embossed bottles with "send me home."

In 1928, Faygo and other Detroit bottlers waged a campaign to get people to return their empties. One ad, in the May 21, 1928, *Detroit Free Press*, urged readers to keep local highways "safe . . . and clean. Every year, thousands upon thousands of bottles are thrown out on the streets and alleys where they become broken, and are a menace to everyone who walks or drives."

To Destroy This Menace

These progressive bottlers are taking this means of placing before the public the necessity of collecting a small deposit through the dealer on all bottles taken from the stores—which of course will be refunded at the time they are returned.

It is assumed that every motorist and the general public will appreciate the concerted effort of these firms to eliminate the glass from our streets, which is so detrimental and costly.

The ad was signed by Faygo and thirty-eight other pop and beer makers and carried an endorsement from the Detroit Automobile Club, which had picked up six tons of glass from highways in 1927. The problem was not to be solved so easily, and discarded bottles became a public nuisance.

For decades, adults returned pop and beer bottles for deposits, and kids made pocket money finding them and taking them to stores. But deposits weren't really working and technology that made cheap nonreturnables was changing the landscape. Bottle litter came up on June 7, 1966, when Councilman William "Billy" Rogell introduced an ordinance to the Detroit City Council to ban throwaway containers by December 31, 1966.

This Faygo logo on this siphon was applied with paint, not embossed. This means it was made by machine, not by hand, and it came after the company's name change around 1920.

Photo credit: Jessica J. Trevino

By 1915, most pop bottles had "crown tops," patented in 1892 by William Painter. The caps look like little crowns and were lined with cork or rubber until plastic liners replaced them around 1970. Crown caps required the invention of bottle openers.

He, like the bottlers' 1928 ad, cited litter and broken glass on streets. Rogell, who served on the city council for almost forty years, was a former major-league baseball player who had supplemented baseball paychecks by delivering bottles of milk.

Mort Feigenson, as secretary of the Metropolitan Detroit Bottlers of Carbonated Beverages, led forty bottlers to a July 7 public hearing on Rogell's proposed ordinance. They argued that a ban on nonreturnables would cost jobs among bottlers and in the glass industry. Rogell said, "I smoked you out. I'm glad to see so many of you. You're making money on these bottles. You ought to spend some of it on education." The bottlers renewed their bring-back-your-empties campaign that month, but changed their focus from litter to clutter. They said 24 million unreturned bottles worth $840,000 were cluttering basements and storage areas. Mort said local pop bottlers were maintaining a "float" of 31 million bottles, up 10 million from 1960. He promised that the bottlers would fund an anti-litter campaign with posters on a thousand trucks and provide thousands of receptacles for empties. The *Detroit Free Press* accompanied the article with a photo of Rogell smoking a pipe and the caption "smoked them out." More smoke was coming.

On January 24, 1967, speaking for Detroit bottlers, Mort again warned about the bottle shortage. He said that people just weren't bringing them back. He said the average pop bottle made 27.2 round trips in 1960, down to 19.6 trips in 1965,

16.9 trips in 1966, and only 15.9 trips by 1967. The industry estimated that 79 percent of bottles were still with customers and only about 8 percent were in stores or on the way to them. The remaining bottles were on their way back to the plant. The *Free Press* reported that Faygo bottles were perilously scarce and that "the big bottle boggle has forced Faygo to step up its promotion of no-deposit bottles and drop deposit bottles altogether outside Detroit." Bottlers, who had once clamored for laws requiring bottles to be returned, now called nonreturnables their key to survival.

In November 1970, Faygo declined to join Coca-Cola and Vernors in increasing deposit fees to bring the bottles in but noted that return rates were at an all-time low. Mort predicted the loss of 320,000 one-quart bottles and said higher deposits in other cities had not increased returns but had prompted a switch to one-way bottles: "We believe the same pattern would hold true in Detroit." Faygo raised its deposit fees in February 1971.

Soon, Faygo pioneered the twist-off bottle cap and one-way plastic containers. Bottlers and grocers did not need to retrieve, wash, and reuse them. Another advantage of twist-off caps was that they could be used to reseal bottles, preserving the fizz.

But nonreturnables were not easily recycled, and they did not solve the litter problem. One design left a metal collar on the neck of the bottle after the cap was twisted off. The rings had to be cut off before the bottles could be recycled. Also, there were problems with consumers not bringing them to recycling centers, breaking them, or not sorting them by color. A 1971 Michigan House bill was designed to require a ten-cent deposit on all bottles and cans and force bottlers to go back to returnables. Mort Feigenson said, "We concede there is a serious problem of solid waste disposal," but he argued for better recycling programs rather than a return to returnables. Other bottlers, grocers, and some unions were on his side.

Faygo pop cans implored, "Please don't litter."

Alarmed that one-use containers would mean more litter and landfills, people in several states campaigned for deposits. The first state to adopt a deposit law was Oregon. Michigan came next.

The Michigan United Conservation Clubs aligned environmentalists and the "hooks and horns" group of sport fishers and hunters. The pro-deposit spokesman was MUCC executive director Tom Washington. The bottlers were represented by Mort Feigenson, Peter Stroh of the Stroh Brewery Company, and Edward Deeb of the grocers' Associated Food Dealers.

The week before the election, all sides came to plead their case before the Detroit City Council, which would decide whether to endorse the proposition.

Feigenson and Stroh warned that their companies could not afford to keep making nonreturnables inside Michigan and sending them off to other states. Feigenson said Faygo would be forced to build outside of Detroit. Stroh said the proposition "will have serious impact on our future plans

A long, expensive fight to defeat a returnable container law in Michigan did not go well for Faygo, Stroh, or merchants. Despite dire predictions for the food and beverage industries, they adapted. So did bottle deposit thieves. *Photo credit: Joe Grimm*

in Detroit. We had hoped to stay in Detroit and double our brewing and shipping capacity."

Unions took the bottlers' side. Michigan AFL-CIO president William Marshall said a bottle law "would send two thousand jobs down the drain." Otis Newsome, president of a union local at a bottling plant, recycled a country song with new lyrics: "When you're runnin' down our union, man, you're walkin' on the fightin' side of me." Washington, however, predicted a mad scramble among bottlers to increase in-state bottle production and distribution. "Stroh's may even have to open a new brewery in Michigan," he said. That was not to be.

On November 2, 1976, voters approved Proposal A. It took effect in December 1978. Did Michigan's bottle law mean doom, a boom, or just a burp?

Early in 1980, Mort told the *Free Press* that 1979 case sales in Michigan had fallen 13.8 percent, while they rose 17.5 percent in the company's nineteen other states. He said 1979 "was the first year ever in which Michigan retailers have not accounted for a majority of total Faygo case sales." He said Faygo earnings were lower than they had been in 1977, but that overall sales were at a record high. The Associated Food Dealers' Deeb said, "Michigan's bottle and can bill is not working because it takes a public nuisance and converts it into a hardship for retailers. The retailer is handling the container three and four times, not just once. We just can't handle this. Why should we be the rubbish collection center for the state of Michigan?"

Michigan's bottle return rate became the highest in the nation at 97 percent. Eight states followed Oregon and Michigan in adopting deposit laws.

Shortly after the new law had been approved, *Detroit Free Press* reporter David Zuchino joshed, "Will we witness the birth of a new petty criminal, the bottlelegger? Visit a dump in, say, Ohio, get a load of empties, put on counterfeit stickers and slip them past Michigan grocery stores?" Eighteen years later, the NBC-TV sitcom *Seinfeld* featured just such a caper. Newman, hoping to collect on Michigan's highest-in-the-nation deposit rate, ten cents, schemed to drive a postal truck full of nonreturnables from New York City to Saginaw, Michigan. Of course, this did not go well. Newman's failure did not discourage a Michigan man in 2016, almost forty years after Zuchino's jest, to truck approximately ten thousand nonrefundable bottles and cans from Kentucky. He was arrested before he could get to the stores. In 2017, a more successful bottlelegger admitted returning in Michigan more than ten thousand nonrefundable cans he had bought as scrap in Indiana and tagged with fake stickers. He was ordered to forfeit truck, trailer, and four hundred thousand dollars.

In 1982, Mort told *Forbes*, "The economic slump had knocked the hell out of Michigan." The company had reported eighty million dollars in sales in 1981, 65 percent outside of Michigan. He said he guessed the company would be in the black again in 1982.

POP Quiz

1. THE OUTLINE ON THE CAP OF SOME PLASTIC FAYGO BOTTLES IS:

A. The Flavor Master's profile
B. West Virginia
C. Ben and Perry's silhouette
D. The Faygo Kid

2. ONE OF THESE LINES APPEARED ON FAYGO TRUCKS. WHICH ONE?

A. Follow the Fizz
B. Which way did he go?
C. Pop the clutch
D. We stop for Redpop

3. WHERE WAS THE FAYGO BOAT SONG COMMERCIAL FILMED?

A. Lake Huron
B. Lake Erie
C. The Detroit River
D. The Pacific Ocean
E. Shasta Lake

4. IN 2014, THE *DETROIT FREE PRESS* REPORTED THAT FAYGO CANS WERE BEING USED:

A. As birdhouses
B. For eavesdropping through walls
C. To alert firefighters to faxed alarms
D. In low-tech telecommunications

5. FOR THE 2008 STANLEY CUP PLAYOFFS, THE MAYOR OF DETROIT BET LOCAL FOODS, INCLUDING FAYGO. PITTSBURGH LOST. WHICH OF THESE WAS NOT PART OF THE BET?

A. Octopus
B. Heinz ketchup
C. Primanti Brothers sandwiches (containing French fries)
D. Pierogies

6. IN JANUARY 1955, FAYGO OFFERED PURCHASERS OF THREE-QUART BOTTLES OF POP:

A. Forty pounds of ice cubes
B. A tour of the factory
C. A paper Faygo hat
D. Glassware

Faygo
People

They Hired Locally

Although Faygo has grown, sending branches throughout the country, it has always remembered its roots.

Susie recalls working at the east-side factory in the summer of 1967. That year, Faygo's sixtieth, civil unrest tore Detroit apart in a frenzy of killing, looting, and arson. The Faygo plant, at 3579 Gratiot Avenue, is on one of the roads that radiate like spokes from the downtown hub of the Motor City. Civil disturbances had damaged Gratiot businesses at least twice before, in 1849 and 1943.

Early in the disturbance, Susie's father prepared to protect his family with a baseball bat and her brother's crossbow, apparently the only weapons they had. One morning that week, she rode to the factory with her dad. National Guard troops and tanks lined Gratiot Avenue, which was littered with burned and looted businesses. Expecting ruins, she was shocked that the plant was undamaged. In August, a newspaper reported

that Faygo had sustained one broken window during the week.

On her father's desk, she said, she saw a list of what looked like IOUs: Jackson, $20; Jones, $15; and so on. She figured her father and Mort had been making loans to people from the neighborhood. However, the Feigensons had not been making just loans. They had been making hires.

According to a card in the newspaper clippings catalog at the Detroit Public Library, the African American newspaper the *Michigan Chronicle* had published a story about Faygo on April 29, 1967. The card noted that Faygo had celebrated an anniversary of its training program and that "60% of male workers are Negroes, 75% of production workers are Negroes."

When the Feigensons moved into their Gratiot Avenue headquarters in 1935, the neighborhood was mostly German and Italian and about 10 percent black. Faygo hired local people. In the late 1940s, after World War II and around the time a second generation of Feigensons was in charge, about one-third of nearby residents were black. The company continued to hire locally and put black drivers on delivery routes, despite some complaints. On the first day of the 1967 disturbances, Lipsky said, 97 percent of Faygo's workers came to work. The company had to send them home.

While Faygo was intact, the stores that sold its pop suffered. The August 11, 1967, *Detroit Jewish News* and the *Free Press* reported that a Faygo survey found that 314 soft-drink outlets had been damaged. Mort reported that 138 sales outlets, or about 2 percent of the 6,200 that Faygo relied on in the Detroit area, and all but a

This 1920 photo from inside the new factory shows seven people at work, including one silhouetted by the back window. By 1938, Faygo employed seventy-five people. *Photo courtesy of the Feigenson family archives*

Despite advances and automation, the pop business still required a lot of lifting. The line of rollers here is like the one in the 1920 factory, but notice the high-low fork tucked under the pallet of cases on the right. *Photo courtesy of the Feigenson family archives*

Two women walk along Detroit's Charlevoix Street with a pack of Faygo cola on August 25, 1967. Three members of the 82nd Airborne Division watch with rifles behind a fence bordering the sidewalk. *Detroit Historical Society/Henri Umbaji King*

few supermarkets were so badly burned that they might never recover. After disturbances in more than a hundred US cities between 1965 and 1967, pop makers began targeting ads directly at the African-American market. Mort, however, told the *Free Press* that Faygo did not discriminate in its advertising. "I realize that the big companies are doing it," he said, "so I'm probably wrong, but that's all right."

In the neighborhood, Faygo was known for treating people fairly. Bill Camp, a black employee hired in March 1937 after being laid off from a foundry job because of a strike at Chrysler,

recalled hearing about an early union-organizing campaign. Camp told the in-house *Faygogazette* in the summer of 1983, "a union was trying to organize Faygo. Mr. [Perry] Feigenson was agreeable. But then he found out that the union contract would require Faygo to get rid of black workers." Camp said Perry told the union, "Go to hell! Faygo hires from the neighborhood around us. And that's how we're going to continue to hire whenever we can."

The unions integrated, and a fiery young Jimmy Hoffa organized a Teamsters union local at Faygo in 1935, Phil told *Free Press* labor writer Ralph Orr. Hoffa was intense. Orr wrote that Phil

White-coated workers move wooden cases, each packed with twelve one-quart bottles of Faygo. In the background, cases are stacked eight layers to a skid and three skids high. Some crates say Uptown and one bears the Faygo shield-and-crown logo. *Photo courtesy of the Feigenson family archives*

recalled "hearing about an argument between Jimmy and a company lawyer, and how Jimmy raised a chair and said, 'Listen, I don't want to hear that crap anymore.' By that time the lawyer was under the desk." Generally, Orr wrote, tables at Faygo were used for negotiating and not as protection. In 1978 Orr wrote, "At the Faygo plant, an inner-city facility with 60 percent of its workers from minority groups, employees put their gripes in writing. They are taken up at the next monthly meeting of a union-management committee and dealt with at once."

Mort said, "If there is static, chances are there is something to it. Problems come more often from management than labor." At the time, Orr reported, Faygo had the highest-paid soft-drink workers in the state, with liberal benefits. He said that when the Feigensons learned that some workers could not read and write, they organized classes. They saw to it that a Vietnam vet received psychiatric care and sent workers with substance abuse problems to drug rehabilitation.

Faygo had a four-month strike in the early 1960s after salesmen objected to being told to load

trucks. There were wildcat strikes in 1968 and 1969 and an official one in 1980. Phil's son Ben, named after his grandfather, recalled, "during a prolonged strike one particularly cold winter, my father gave orders to break up some of the wooden pallets to provide firewood for the men on the picket line." Ben recalled that the Faygo contract required that workers be dismissed if their wages were garnisheed three times: "This happened to a particular employee and my father went out of his way to find him another job at a bottler in Indianapolis." Ben also said that his father paid off the mortgage of a worker who died during a strike so the worker's family would not lose its home.

Mort's 1972 holiday message for the in-house employee *Faygogazette* described the "mighty depressing experience" of the daily news in the papers and on TV. When concerns got to him, he wrote, he would "take a walk into our bottle shop and watch the men at work. Almost always I see things which make me feel better. I see men of various backgrounds and religions, black and white, working together in obvious good spirits. Differences seem to be forgotten and everyone is cooperating to get the job done. Almost every day I see men do small things for a fellow employee that they could avoid doing if they chose. I am sure these little things are noted and appreciated."

In 1977, for Faygo's seventieth anniversary, *Detroit Free Press* columnist Frank Angelo visited the Feigensons. Mort told him, "Our fathers and we believe that you provide neighborhood people with the jobs that need to be filled." With 320 employees, Faygo was one of the largest employers in Detroit, Angelo wrote, and most of its workers were from its predominantly black neighborhood. Mort said, "It took us some time to catch on to what all the affirmative action talk was all about because we had been doing it quite naturally for years. Actually, we had dropped some customers and others dropped us because they were upset when we first started using black drivers for our delivery trucks many years ago."

. . . And People Stayed

The company, which was run by just two generations of Feigensons for eighty years, prided itself on the long tenure of its employees. Faygo's founders ran the company for forty years. Then, cousins Morton and Phil ran it for almost forty more. They hired several people who stayed for decades, a few even longer than the owners did. This gave Faygo direct lines back to its beginnings in 1907, with very few changes in command or philosophy.

Harvey Lipsky, known as Mr. Faygo, the company's unofficial historian, joined the company as a chemist in 1958 and stayed for more than fifty years, retiring at age 76. He learned Feigensonian values directly from co-founder Perry, who lived until 1964.

In 2016, Al Chittaro was named president of Faygo Beverages. He had started with the company as a part-time driver in his teens in the late 1970s, when Mort and Phil ran the company.

Harvey Lipsky started at Faygo as a chemist and stayed for more than fifty years. He became known as the company's unofficial historian and acquired the sobriquets "Mr. Faygo" and "chief elixir mixer."

Photo credit: Lipsky Family photo

After choosing Chittaro, National Beverage Corp. chairman and CEO Nick A. Caporella said, "Al is as much a part of Faygo—as Faygo is of Detroit, starting as a teenager working part time as a driver/salesman. Detroit and Faygo both have earned iconic status in early American industry development. From soda pioneering to soft drink innovation, Faygo today is a Liberty Bell symbol that has survived and progressed as a hallmark within the soft drink industry." One of Ben Feigenson's grandsons, Matt Rosenthal, started by working summers as a student in the syrup room. He told the *Free Press*, "I would get on the bus to go home

and no one would sit next to me. I had to take a shower just so I could take a shower. So sweet!" Rosenthal eventually became marketing director and was with Faygo until he was sixty-eight.

Longevity was not just a privilege of the bosses.

In 1966, to serve its expanding markets, Faygo hired Bruce Scott as its first over-the-road driver. Scott was key in delivering pop to food chains and wholesalers, rather than making store-door deliveries. A 1984 issue of the in-house *Faygogazette* lauded Scott for two million miles "remarkably free of chargeable-to-him accidents."

The *Faygogazette* explained that when over-the-road drivers roll out, they are responsible for as much as a hundred thousand dollars in equipment and cargo. Scott usually handled the assignment perfectly. There was just this one day in June of 1974. Coming back from Syracuse with a load of empty bottles, something happened just after dawn on a clear, dry morning. The next thing he knew, the trailer and its cargo were totaled. The tractor had four thousand dollars in damage. Scott, wearing a seat belt, suffered only minor head injuries. Without witnesses, Scott's story to Faygo executives would be the explanation. Scott admitted, "I fell asleep at the wheel."

The in-house organ said, "Faygo management, in a final review of Bruce's case, concluded that the six words Bruce had uttered constituted more than an explanation of a deplorable accident, that the words also projected the everyday posture of a man of unusual character, character impossible of not being admired and respected. Thus, Bruce was

Filled bottles zip past Mort and Phil to find their labels in 1973. That year, Faygo recommitted to Detroit's east side with a million-dollar expansion that would help make more one way bottles. *Photo credit: Detroit Free Press*

not fired. He was, however, given a suspension from which he came back to be a more valued than ever employee."

The same issue profiled Matt Ingram, a thirty-one-year Faygo man who had just a grade-school education. He said, "Yazoo, Mississippi, where I was born, was not a place where taxpayers were willing to have their taxes used to educate black children. The people who had the say there figured black kids were best off working in the fields." Ingram, then fifty-six and a label machine operator, started working at Faygo before civil rights legislation opened up schools and when

drinking fountains, bathrooms, and other public amenities were segregated.

According to the *Faygogazette*, "Though he very much likes working at Faygo, a 'company man' he is definitely not. . . . 'Nobody is stronger for the union than I am,' contends Matt. 'But, as a union man, I also know that the worst Faygo could do to its employees would be to operate the company so as not to make any profits. No profits, no jobs. It's as simple as that.'" Ingram boasted that he had never been laid off or suspended. Another long-tenured Faygo driver was former employee Herman Polk, who sent the Feigenson family a card printed with the words, "Thank you and bless you for being so nice." Polk picked it up from there: " . . . to me and my family while working for you from 1953 to 1983. May God bless you and your family, may all your holidays be blessed, Love you."

An item in the August 16, 1983, *Free Press* said, "Bruce Sharp Jr., the 2 1/2-year-old Commerce Township tyke suffering from a congenital liver ailment that's expensive to treat, had a great weekend. Fund-raising events in his behalf in Novi raised $50,000 and better yet, dad Bruce Sr., an unemployed steel worker, was hired by Faygo soft drinks. Young Bruce's malady requires extensive therapeutic trips to Pittsburgh for a transplant, whenever a suitable donor is found."

Orr, the labor reporter, wrote that for its seventieth anniversary, the company entrusted an employee group with planning the celebration— and gave it a twenty-five-thousand-dollar budget. The party was held November 1 at the cousins' favorite restaurant, Joe Muer's. A few days before Orr's article ran, word had gotten around the neighborhood that Faygo would be hiring. Two hundred people applied.

Many Faygo workers rose through the ranks. Lee Skelton, Faygo's labor relations director, told Orr that the production manager had once been a foreman and that the transportation and sales managers had started out as truck drivers.

In 1997, Lipsky told the *Detroit News,* "This place is my life." And then, he stayed for ten more years.

Citizen Faygo

This eight-ounce bottle says Bull Dog Ginger Beer Co. on the bottom and Wolverine Ginger Ale Co. on the back. Some old-timers swear they used to buy it at Atlas.

Venerable Vernors had its start in Detroit in 1866, more than forty years before Faygo started. Vernors left in 1985, after 119 years.

Competition was strong among the dozens of brands and bottlers that bubbled away in Detroit's pop alley. The brands that Faygo and its competitors produced created a vibrant neighborhood industry. However, Faygo prevailed by becoming part of the larger community. The Feigensons' loyalty to Detroit's near east side was evident in scholarships, neighborhood improvement, and where the Feigensons lived. Faygo was more than just another bottling company. Faygo was also a citizen.

From the beginning, when one small frame building was both home and factory, the Feigensons were Detroiters. As their business and families outgrew the little house at Hastings and Benton, they found bigger quarters and homes. They lived in some of Detroit's best neighborhoods: Boston-Edison, Palmer Woods, Lafayette Park.

Susie Feigenson recalls, "When I went to school, I went to James Vernor Elementary, and I felt very guilty because they gave Vernors and candy canes at Christmas, and how dare I drink the Vernors and have those candy canes? I was the competition." The school was, in fact, named for her father's competitor, who also had a street named for him, not far from the Faygo plant.

At times, even in later years, a Feigenson lived close enough to walk to work. They were invested in the city figuratively and literally. They put money into their city and country, education, the arts, health, history, and Jewish causes. Beginning in 1928 and continuing for many years, the Feigensons sponsored the top prize, a gold medal, for scholars at Hebrew schools. The medal became known as the Feigenson Medal. When World War II came, the Feigensons supported and promoted war bond drives and joined food merchant committees to support the war effort. In the ultimate act of citizenship, three sons joined the thousands of Jews from Detroit who enlisted.

Shaken by his brother's death at age 28, Herman made a $3,333 donation in 1958 to establish

The pixie-branded caramel cream root beer was probably the best-known pop of Atlas Bottling. It sold nationally for a while. Atlas closed, and Brownie, complete with the pixie mascot, is now produced by retro bottler Orca Beverage, Inc., in Mukilteo, Washington.

These caps for Faygo's Uptown seem to present a mystery. The yellow one says Vernors and Hersey, Michigan. The green one says Holly Beverage Co., and Youngstown, Ohio. Keith Wunderlich, who has studied and written about Vernors for years, said bottlers frequently agreed to produce others' products.

would be expected to buy Faygo. The company started a program to put parolees from the neighborhood back to work in its plant. Faygo helped with neighborhood beautification, opened its first-aid station to neighborhood children, and, in 1972, started giving five-hundred-dollar scholarships and summer jobs to students at three high schools near the plant. Mort said, "The old man used to say, 'You've got to be a good neighbor,' so we work at it. It goes back a long way."

a scholarship in Albert's name for Wayne State University English and music students. Another scholarship, named for Perry and Herman, goes to Wayne State science students.

Before the violence of 1967, which prompted other businesses to re-examine their relations with the community, Faygo was already involved. Lipsky told the *Free Press*, "we went out and asked to join the local block club." People asked if they

Mort's wife, Jackie, became deeply involved in Detroit's art scene, supporting young painters and sculptors at her Feigenson Gallery in Detroit's Fisher Building. In a 1979 interview, she said, "There is a quality to the art produced in Detroit that speaks of Detroit. It's tough, sometimes harsh, but the energy is there." The acting director of the Detroit Institute of Arts, Michael Kan, said, "She supported her artists with warmth and understanding, and she let Detroiters know that there is a great deal that's worthwhile right here at their back door." She died in 1984.

Mort and Jackie Feigenson supported the Allied Jewish Campaign, the United Negro College

Grilli Brothers Beverage Co. was one of dozens of pop makers clustered in Detroit in the early half of the 1900s. It was owned by Alberto Grilli, according to *Italians in Detroit*. Its last address was about three miles north of Faygo's current plant.

Fund, and the Michigan Council for the Arts. The year before he died, Mort was elected to the board of his neighborhood co-op.

Faygo investment has continued under new owners. Working with companies in the Associated Food Dealers, now the Associated Food and Petroleum Dealers, Faygo has given away turkeys for the holidays, merchandise, and, of course, lots and lots of Faygo. Faygo began an academic all-star scholarship contest in 1999 and in 2005 awarded scholarships to students in the city and suburbs in a black history essay contest. In 2003, Faygo dressed up its strip of Gratiot with a new 11,500-square-foot façade, including two hundred new feet of sidewalk and street. It was accompanied by a $2,500 donation to the Detroit Police Foundation and a tent party. Stan Sheridan said "renovating the façade and the sign on our building symbolizes our recommitment to the City of Detroit."

Susie said her father, Phil, told her: "Always be grateful that you are in a position to give." In Mort's obituary, his niece, Sydelle Sonkin, said: "They were always supporters of the city. They believed that the city nurtured you, and you nurtured the city."

Ace Hy was Faygo's 1920s answer to the Chero-Cola's Nehi line, including many fruit flavors, a cola, a chocolate, and more. Chero-Cola rebranded its most successful flavor as Royal Crown Cola, and it became the name of the company. At one time, Nehi and Faygo were pop alley neighbors.

POP Quiz

1. WHAT WAS THE ORIGINAL NAME OF DR FAYGO POP?

A. Mr Faygo
B. Twenty-three
C. Faygo Pepper
D. Dr Mort
E. Doctorade

2. FAYGO SPONSORED THE 1954 SCREEN RELEASE OF *THE CAINE MUTINY* BY:

A. Releasing balloons from Detroit's Madison Theatre
B. Holding a boat race on the Detroit River
C. Giving away Faygo sailor hats
D. Launching a saltwater taffy pop

3. DETROIT-BORN NATIONAL BASKETBALL LEAGUE PLAYER CHRIS DOUGLAS-ROBERTS HAD THE FAYGO LOGO TATTOOED ON HIS:

A. Shooting hand
B. Tummy
C. Shoulder
D. Neck

4. AN ATHLETE NICKNAMED "RED POP" PLAYED FOR:

A. The Lions
B. The Red Wings
C. The Tigers
D. The Pistons

5. WHICH CELEBRITY DID NOT ADVERTISE FAYGO?

A. Fighter Tommy Hearns
B. Football player Alex Karras
C. Actress Joan Rivers
D. Actor Jamie Farr
E. Baseball player Darryl Strawberry

6. WHICH PUPPETEER HELPED PITCH FAYGO?

A. Jim Henson
B. Shari Lewis
C. Edgar Bergen and Charlie McCarthy
D. Señor Wences

Street Marketing

Faygo had to fight for attention in the word-of-mouth, hand-to-hand world of pop alley. One of the company's first big decisions was its 1920 move to shorten Feigenson Brothers Bottling Co. to Faygo, which fit better on pop bottles. Faygo is shorter and snappier, though another good choice might have been "Ben and Perry's."

One of Faygo's earliest campaigns was on trucks, which greatly expanded its distribution range from horse-and-wagon days. Many companies had their names lettered in gold or white on their trucks and photographed them in front of the factory or office. Trucks represented investment, innovation, permanence. After the size of fleets came to represent success, Phil had truck trailers painted different colors on opposite sides. Passersby who saw a red truck going up the street and a blue truck coming back had no idea

they were seeing the same truck, painted to look like two.

The family helped with the marketing. Susie Feigenson recalled, "Many times when the family would be together . . . usually on Sunday morning, we would be shopping together for Sunday brunch, and we would go into a supermarket, and we'd move all the Faygo to the middle shelves. Whatever had been there—Coke, Pepsi—we would change things so we would be at eye level. You want to be where you can catch that eye." She also said Phil would learn where owners of potential sales outlets lived and overstock the stores along the streets between their homes and stores. Phil hoped that, when the potential customer saw how available Faygo was all along the way, he would sign up. At the stores, Faygo used modest point-of-purchase advertising, with signs in store doors and windows, labeled racks for Faygo, and lighted clocks. One three-shelf unit had inserts with the Faygo logo and a single word in blue on each insert: "Partytime," "Mealtime," "Anytime."

A four-shelf unit had these catchphrases: "Peps Up Party-Time"; "Refreshes TV-Time"; "Brightens Mealtime"; "Delicious Anytime."

Outdoor signs displayed the Faygo logo and the name of the store. Faygo had advertising murals painted on exterior walls of stores and other buildings. Companies advertised tobacco, beer, pop, packaged food, and other products. Scrubbed by rain and faded by sun, some became ghost signs. Others, covered when another

Susie Feigenson keeps her father's simple nameplate in her home. It accompanies this desk model of a Faygo truck painted red on the left side and blue on the right. *Photo credit: Jessica J. Trevino*

Faygo flagged the locations where its pops were for sale with high-visibility signs at well-located beverage outlets. *Photo credit: Rick McOmber*

This ad was painted on a bar in the Detroit suburb of Warren to advertise Faygo Uptown. This is how the ad looked on August 25, 2007, after sixty years of weathering. Ten years later, the sign was almost entirely gone. *Photo credit: Derek and Kerry Farr/DetroitDerek Photography*

building was built right up against them, survived for decades, like narrow time capsules.

About sixty miles northeast of Detroit, muralist Steve Nordgren restored most of an Uptown sign. He said the owner of a three-story building where he had once owned a sign company commissioned him to restore it. Nordgren said, "We did a lot of research and pulled up various logos from that time period and found something that was very close to what was on there, and we came close to repainting what was the original."

When Henry Ford put people on wheels, billboards gave them something to look at.

When Faygo circulated its "refreshability" signs, it was taking a shot at Coca-Cola, which had been promoting refreshment for years. According

This "party store," as Detroiters call them, had Faygo signs facing Euclid and Fort Streets and bottles of Faygo in all the windows. A sign in the window advertised three one-quart bottles for a quarter. *Photo courtesy of the Feigenson family archives*

to *Advertising Age*, Coke's first tagline was "Delicious and refreshing" in 1886, the year it was invented. Coke went on to use "Refresh Yourself" (1924); "The Pause that Refreshes" (1929); "Be Really Refreshed" (1959); and "Refreshment." The only keywords that show up more often are "Taste" and "Real." An ad, from Coca-Cola's fortieth anniversary in 1926 shows five variations of "refresh." Who can blame Faygo for tweaking Coke? Susie said a family story is that Coca-Cola once asked her grandfather, Ben, if he wanted to be regional manager for the company. His reply, with a Russian accent: "What kind of name is Coca-Cola?"

While signs brought Faygo to street corners, the new medium of TV brought it right into people's homes.

Cartoons, Kids, and Celebs

Faygo TV commercials had their roots in 1935 when the brothers entrusted a two-thousand-dollar advertising budget to Julian Grace, a thirty-two-year-old ad man who worked as a one-man agency for Faygo for several years. When Grace joined the W. B. Doner & Co. agency in 1943, he brought Faygo

The restoration of a Port Huron Uptown sign was only partial because, as often happens to advertising murals, another building was built right in front of it. *Photo credit: Joe Grimm*

Urban photographer Nailhead wrote that he traveled McGraw almost daily to avoid freeway tie-ups. On August 1, 2012, he saw that a building was being renovated and its siding had been pulled off. He said he saw the ad and stopped immediately. *Photo credit: Nailhead.com*

The mural, complete with fruit slices and lions framing a Faygo crest, was brought back to light for just one day. The next day, Nailhead reported, it was under cover again. *Photo credit: Nailhed.com*

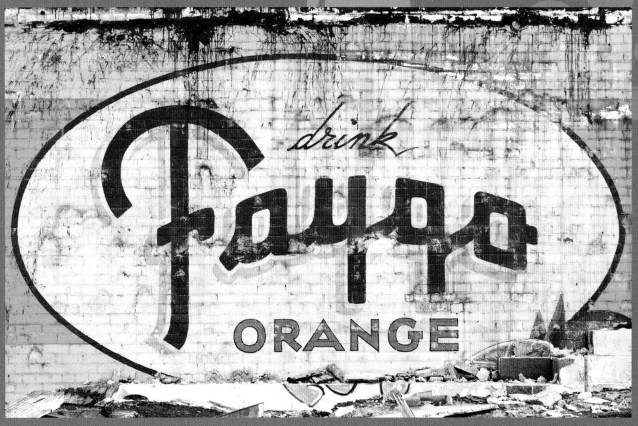

This ghost sign, bearing a logo used from the 1930s to the 1950s, was hidden for years by a store built right up against it at Mt. Elliott Street and Georgia Street on the city's east side. It was exposed after the adjacent building burned and was torn down in 2012. Photos were taken as late as October, 2013, but vandals defaced the sign with paint, ruining it. *Photo credit: James C. Ritchie*

After the discovery and then destruction of the Faygo orange mural, Jordan Zielke and Kelly Golden of Golden Sign Co. were hired to recreate it on the Faygo plant about four miles south of where the sign was found. The painters met while students at the University of Michigan and started their company about the time the original mural was uncovered. *Photo credit: Jordan Zielke*

With its home high on the northeast end of Faygo's building on Gratiot, behind a fence and with little chance that a building will go up right next to it, this ghost found a new life. Zielke and Golden also painted a smaller replica of the sign in a bar. *Photo credit: Jordan Zielke*

This billboard connected Faygo to factory work during World War II, in which the next generation of Faygo leaders served. President Franklin D. Roosevelt called US wartime factories "the greatest arsenal of democracy." *Photo courtesy of the Detroit Historical Society*

Faygo signs proclaiming its cola's "refreshability" were a direct response to Coca-Cola's longtime claims to refreshment. Susie Feigenson keeps this sign in her garage.

with him. Doner, founded by Brod Doner in the recessionary year of 1937, was small. It grew by bringing in salespeople like Grace who worked "vest pocket" accounts. They kept their autonomy and shared resources. Early Doner clients included brewers, a chandelier company, and a burlesque theater.

To Doner and the second generation of Faygo owners, TV gleamed like an opportunity. In 1951, when only 23.5 percent of American homes had television sets, Faygo sponsored *The Laurel and Hardy Show* on pioneering WXYZ-TV. In December 1952, Faygo picked up sponsorship of the 1953 TV series *Boston Blackie* after a ten-day visit to Hollywood by Mort Feigenson and Julian Grace to make commercials and shop for shows. In 1953, comedian Soupy Sales debuted on Detroit's WXYZ-TV. In three more years, the proportion of TV-watching homes more than doubled. In another three years, TV ownership had tripled to

This 1947 ground-level billboard was part of the series that included the double cola one. The boy is pouring Faygo strawberry, rebranded about fifteen years later as Redpop. *Photo courtesy of the Feigenson family archives*

Kent Taylor played Boston Blackie opposite Lois Collier as Mary in a TV show from 1951 to 1954. During a visit with the actors in 1952, Whitie, who played their dog, jumped into Mort Feigenson's arms. *Photo courtesy of the Feigenson family archives*

Stan Laurel and Oliver Hardy retired in 1950 and made only one television appearance after that. However, Faygo sponsored their comedies on TV and used impressionists of the comedy duo in a Redpop commercial.

Comedian Soupy Sales hosted the largely ad-libbed noontime Detroit TV show *Lunch with Soupy Sales*. Its mix of cream pies in the face and risqué jokes attracted kids and adults.

"The Faygo Kid" was such a classic commercial that people remembered and asked for it years later. It put Faygo and W. B. Doner and Co. advertising agency ahead of their peers in TV's early days. *Photo courtesy of the Feigenson family archives*

Late in 1972, Faygo reprised the seventeen-year-old Faygo Kid and Black Bart commercial for a week on two Detroit stations. The idea came out of a conversation between a Faygo exec and a New York customer who asked whatever happened to the commercial.

78.6 percent of homes. As TV grew, so did Faygo's investment in advertising.

The early 1950s were a turning point for Doner, Faygo, TV, and cartoon animation. The first postwar census put the city's population at 1.86 million, making it the fifth largest city in the country. Doner, which had been using radio, broke into national prominence with its TV campaigns for Faygo, Tavern Pale Beer, and Speedway 79 gasoline. Doner's first TV commercials for Faygo were black-and-white. The partnership elevated Faygo and Doner's reputations, and some say TV commercials helped animation survive and cross over from the big screen to the small one's ads and Saturday morning cartoons.

In the 1950s, animators were throwing off the Disney-driven character design of ball, egg, and pear shapes strung on midlines and using more modern techniques, more motion, and minimalism. Doner commissioned several character-driven commercials for Faygo. The best known

was the 1956 Faygo Kid, in which the black-hatted Black Bart holds up the "Wells Faygo Express" stagecoach for its old-fashioned Faygo root beer. The Faygo Kid, in a white hat, assures the maiden in the coach that he will save the root beer, and does. The commercial's tagline was, "Which way did he go, which way did he go?" Black Bart's horse answered: "He went for Fayg-o-o-o!" The commercial was so popular it is now in the American Advertising Federation's hall of fame, and Faygo took out newspaper ads telling people when it would air. There was an actual Black Bart who was notorious for robbing Wells Fargo stagecoaches from 1875 to 1883, but he was afraid of horses. Phil Feigenson's daughter Susie said that her family named their Doberman Black Bart.

John Hubley at Playhouse Pictures in Hollywood directed "The Faygo Kid," which was animated by Art Babbitt and cost nine thousand dollars to produce. Playhouse did work for most of the Hanna-Barbera cartoons and commercials,

Artist David Weidman created this concept painting for Faygo's bluesy black cherry commercial, and he made the little boy in overalls black. In the commercial, the children are all white. Working with John Hubley, Weidman was a pioneer of the stylized backgrounds of mid-twentieth-century modernism. His credits include work in *Mr. Magoo's Christmas Carol* and *Popeye*. *Illustration courtesy of Lenna Weidman, trustee of the David Weidman and Dorothy Weidman Living Trust*

including *The Flintstones*, *The Jetsons*, *Care Bears*, and *Scooby-Doo*. Television also helped Hubley over a rough patch. Hubley had left Disney during a 1941 strike and, because of his activism, was caught up in the Red Scare of the 1950s. This cost him a job as creative director at an animation studio and forced the cancellation of an animated adaptation of a Broadway play he was working on.

Hubley is credited with an elegant 1955 commercial featuring a bluesy soundtrack with the lyrics "Faygo black cherry. Get your Faygo black cherry today." In it, a pushcart Faygo vendor, seeing two boys tease a girl who does not have money to buy a cup of black cherry as they did, flips her a coin so she can buy a whole bottle for herself.

Playhouse also produced a commercial for Uptown pop, featuring Herkimer Bottleneck, who

Bottles were so central to Faygo that even decades after they were no longer blown by hand, the star of one Uptown commercial was Herkimer the pop-bottle blower. When he became "too pooped to participate" and created a bottleneck on the line, his foreman suggested he get "up, up, up with Uptown." The script for this twenty-four-panel Uptown storyboard survived, but the characters did not. They kept their names, Lothario and Grace, but were redrawn at Playhouse Pictures as a French couple in a big city. It seems unlikely the commercial was ever finished or aired. *Illustrations from Playhouse Pictures*

was blowing bottles on a line in a pop factory. Herkimer becomes exhausted blowing ninety one-quart bottles an hour and says he is "too pooped to participate." His foreman tells him to "Blow, or go," and gives him a bottle of Uptown, which perks him right up and has him blowing bottles again in no time. Herkimer's foreman was voiced by Thurl Ravenscroft, who also did Tony the Tiger saying, "They're gr-r-reat!" for Kellogg's Frosted Flakes. Ravenscroft's bass provided voices and singing in hundreds of commercials, shorts, films, TV shows, Disney rides, and video games from 1939 to 1999. His TV credits included the original *Dr. Seuss' How the Grinch Stole Christmas*, *The Lorax*, and *The Hobbit*. While "Herkimer" was Uptown's signature commercial, at least two other Uptown TV ads were attempted.

An unsigned twenty-four-panel Playhouse Pictures storyboard sketches out an Uptown commercial featuring a fez-wearing Lothario Burke and his love interest, Grace, in harem pants and veil. The clothing and arches place it in Arabia. It seems never to have been produced, the sketches snatched off a board so that the pins holding the panels tore them. However, the script was used in a rough animation that placed Lothario and Grace in a city, gave them French accents, and put Lothario in a beret and ascot.

In 1958 and 1959, before Muppet-maker Jim Henson made it big with *Sesame Street*, he was making things small in hundreds of eight-second TV commercials. Ten were for Faygo. Henson created the short commercials for station identification spots, which were ten seconds long. This

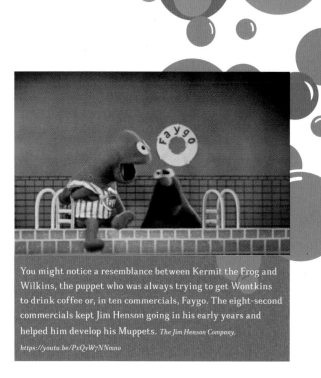

You might notice a resemblance between Kermit the Frog and Wilkins, the puppet who was always trying to get Wontkins to drink coffee or, in ten commercials, Faygo. The eight-second commercials kept Jim Henson going in his early years and helped him develop his Muppets. *The Jim Henson Company.* https://youtu.be/PxQvW7NNmno

allowed an eight-second story and a two-second product shot. Story lines were simple and violent. Most were for Wilkins Coffee in the Washington, DC, market. The stars were a Kermit-like Muppet named Wilkins and a blobby-looking Wontkins. Usually, the cheery Wilkins tried to get the grumpy Wontkins to drink the coffee. Wontkins wouldn't, of course, and usually ended up getting hurt. Commercials featured a buzz saw, cannon, electric chair, hammer, handgun, and other sado-comedic devices. Some commercials closed with the line "Things just seem to happen to people who don't drink Wilkins." In a Faygo spot, Wilkins is sitting poolside and says, "I just filled my whole swimming pool with Faygo strawberry." Wontkins falls in and cries, "Help, I'm drowning!" Wilkins: "I told him he'd end up drinking Faygo." Henson made the commercials for other coffee companies, bread companies, and more. In *Of Muppets and Men:*

Harold Peary created a spinoff hit for NBC and then did it again with Faygo, spinning from shopkeeper to song leader. One story says he was signed because Mort Feigenson liked a schmaltzy Great Gildersleeve pitching Redpop, recorded as a joke.

"Here's 50¢ from Faygo!"

Faygo used the image of Peary in an outfit similar to the one in the Boat Song commercial in a promotional campaign that sent half dollars to customers.

Image courtesy Ed Golick/detroitkidshow.com

The Making of the Muppet Show, Henson said, "'Till then, advertising agencies believed that the hard sell was the only way to get their message over on television. We took a very different approach. We tried to sell things by making people laugh."

Spurred by the need to promote its diet flavors to adults, and rebranding strawberry as Redpop, Faygo had a second golden age of commercials in the late '60s and 1970s. Faygo's 1970 ad budget was one million dollars. The Boat Song commercial, contrary to popular belief, was not made on a Boblo boat. Faygo originally planned to shoot the commercial in the summer of 1973 with people singing "Remember When You Were a Kid" on one of the Detroit River boats. But Faygo wanted the commercial ready for summer, so production was moved several months earlier, and to a warmer setting. They found it off Acapulco, Mexico, aboard the tour boat *Fiesta*.

The commercial's star was comedian and singer Harold Peary, who had appeared on radio, in films and animations, and on TV. His breakout character was Throckmorton P. Gildersleeve, a character on the *Fibber McGee and Molly* NBC Red Network radio comedy. Peary's character gave rise to the Great Gildersleeve, the first spinoff hit in US broadcasting.

As he directed the crowd on the *Fiesta*, they sang "Remember When You Were a Kid," written by Ed Labunski and sung by jingle writer Kenny Karen. The song, set to a waltz, embodied childhood memories and innocence. Peary also played a grocer in a mom-and-pop store. In one

In December 1973, Faygo's Art Rosenthal wrote in the company's *Faygogazette*, "This year's advertising was unquestionably our most successful since the 'Faygo Kid' in 1956. . . . We received hundreds of letters and phone calls telling us what a beautiful commercial we created. The song was made available at 25 cents, and we sold over 42,000! It made the top 40 on radio stations across the country." Sales ultimately reached 75,000.

Auntie Dee

Some of Faygo's first steps into TV were as a sponsor of early TV kids' shows. Here, they bring Dee Parker, "Auntie Dee," host of a kiddie talent show, to the table with comic legends Laurel and Hardy, whose show they also sponsored. *Image courtesy Ed Golick/detroitkidshow.com*

commercial, one little boy and then another ask, "What flavors ya got?" Peary gets exasperated listing all of Faygo's flavors. Then an adult asks the same question, but in sugar-free flavors. All the recitations conclude with "Redpop," and that's what they all order. In a variation, Laurel and Hardy actors run through the same routine, and also order Redpop. Thin-man Laurel asks for regular Redpop. Heavyset Hardy asks for sugar-free diet. The act concludes, of course, with them bumbling into each other, knocking over displays of Faygo cans, and falling on the floor. Hardy tells a head-scratching Laurel, "This is another fine mess you've gotten me into." A can of Redpop conks Hardy on the head. Laurel notes, "I think that

was regular." The announcer asks, "When was the last time you had a good slug?" In one commercial, the shopper is played by Detroit Lions Hall of Famer Alex Karras, who had become an actor in movies and on TV. He became a spokesman for the low-calorie line.

The slightly daffy defensive tackle was a contrast to Faygo's 1968 commercials for Frosh, aimed at adults. In them, an impressionist imitating the boozy voice of cigar-smoking actor W. C. Fields says, "Frosh is for grownups. Yes, indeed. Low-calorie Frosh by Faygo in handy no-return bottles. Any soft drink that's not made for small children can't be all bad." Fields, who died in 1946, was characterized as taking kids into bars but refusing

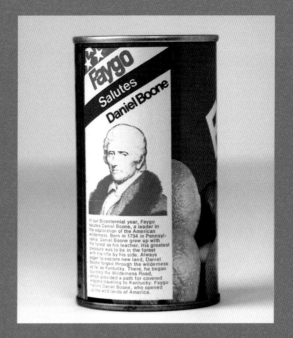

W. C. Fields never made a commercial for Faygo, but impressionists who could capture his snide mumble and bleary look made him a spokesman for the adult-aimed Frosh. Fields' tastes ran to adult beverages of the alcoholic type. Here he is in the 1935 film *David Copperfield*. Fields died on Christmas Day 1946.

In the 1970s, when US Bicentennial fever was high, Faygo ran several series of cans recognizing American achievements. They included salutes to individuals and milestones in different industries.

to work with them or small animals. Humorist Leo Rosten praised Fields by saying, "Any man who hates dogs and babies can't be all bad." Sometimes, people misattribute the quote to Fields.

The voice played over video of a billiard player, a takeoff on a Fields comedy routine. The player on the commercial was national billiards champion Jimmy Caras shooting trick shots. The real trick had been finding the right voice. *Detroit Free Press* columnist Bob Talbert wrote on August 19, 1968, that Doner vice president Skip Roberts had said, "We wanted to do a soft-drink commercial for adults. We needed something different to get Frosh over as an adult soft drink. What better than W. C. Fields?"

Talbert wrote that Doner "gathered 140 impressions of Fields. No one was just right. By

luck, Doner found a Hollywood animator, Bill Oberlin, who did Fields impressions at night-clubs as a side hustle." Oberlin was a challenge, Roberts told Talbert: "Oberlin couldn't read the lines. He froze. He panicked. He fluffed lines. He blew them—he was just impossible. . . . In all, nine hours of taping and recording to get five minutes of commercials." The work paid off, however. The January 30, 1969, *Free Press* declared, "Hottest advertising agency in the country . . . their W. C. Fields pool table commercial for Faygo Frosh named as one of the year's finest." Faygo also used Detroit's "King of Korn," Karrell Fox, who played Milky the Clown on Detroit TV kids' programs, in some Fields commercials, according to the *Free Press* and Detroit kids TV historian Ed Golick.

The Faygo rainbow was not just a catchy coincidence. It was part of a canny plan to beat big one-flavor soda companies with variety. In 1977, Mort Feigenson gave people something to read and think about while they drank.

Faygo kept bringing Karras back. In a 1970 commercial, he is devouring a pizza all by himself.

ANNOUNCER: "Hey, um, Alex. Alex? I thought you were on a diet."

KARRAS: "I am on a diet. See? Faygo sugar-free Redpop. Boy, nobody makes diet pop as good as Faygo."

ANNOUNCER: "Yeah, but Alex, what about the pizza?"

KARRAS: Pauses, smiles: "Faygo doesn't make pizza."

In 1971, Faygo flew Karras to Hollywood to do another series of commercials for sugar-free pops with Peary. But Faygo soon wanted something fresh and benched Karras.

By 1976, swept up in its ambitions for national expansion, Faygo ended more than thirty years with Doner. Faygo's advertising budget had grown

When Alex Karras became a Faygo pitchman, he was already having success in TV and films. His 1974 credits included Mongo in *Blazing Saddles*.

Hearns' companion Gino Linder used a straw to blow bubbles into the bottle after each shot. The heat of the lights made the punch lose its fizz. *Photo credit: Ira Rosenberg for the* Detroit Free Press

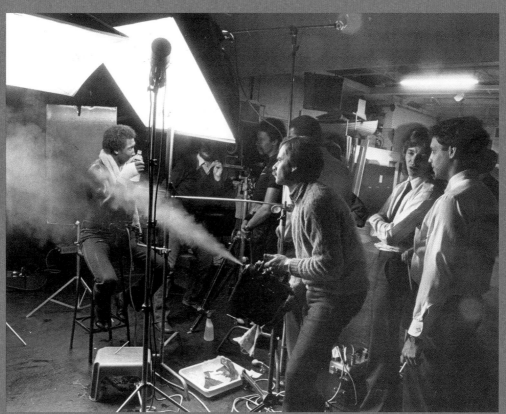

When Tommy "Hitman" Hearns was photographed for a Faygo punch campaign, white light illuminated him and the bottle, and blue lights illuminated his hair. Mist simulated sweat, and "bug juice" fogged the background. The tiny east-side studio smelled bad, but the picture worked. *Photo credit: Ira Rosenberg for the* Detroit Free Press

from $2,000 when it started with Julian Grace to $2 million. Mort told the *Detroit News*:

> Doner did a fantastic job. They created classic ads for us for thirty years, back to the Faygo Kid. What happened is that Doner put Faygo out in front in TV. We stayed ahead for years and finally Coke and Pepsi caught up with us. They've come on real strong in the last four or five years and the game changed and we felt we had to change. Doner felt right to the end we didn't have to change—and that's where we came to a parting of the ways.

However, Faygo did not abandon TV with its new agencies.

The largely wordless late-1970s commercial "Monkey Business" was filmed at the Detroit Zoo and starred animals. In it, a monkey drinks a distracted father's Faygo as his son looks on. The father winds up ordering replacements—for all three of them. Cue the announcer: "You can't say no to Faygo." Another commercial promoted Faygo's rainbow of thirty-three flavors with young people painting a rainbow.

In a 1979 commercial Faygo probably wanted to get back, *M*A*S*H* actor Jamie Farr wears a feathered headdress and says that Redpop was a gift to thirsty native people from the great spirit Faygo. After five firms in five years, Faygo went back with Doner in 1980. The agency picked up where it had left off, hiring nationally known comedian Joan Rivers to do commercials for diet Faygo. *Funding Universe* wrote that Rivers' fee was high, but "the expense was approved by Mort Feigenson, and the spots did well for the firm. Feigenson prided himself on getting the most for his advertising dollar, and was insistent on making Faygo's ads look as good as those of national competitors such as Coke and Pepsi."

In one commercial, Rivers and actress Paula Warner compare their figures over diet Frosh. In another, Rivers is dining at a fancy restaurant and complains that, although she ordered diet Faygo root beer, the waiter must have served her regular.

In 1983, Faygo signed boxer Tommy Hearns, whom *Detroit News* columnist Terry Foster called Detroit's fifth sports team after the Lions, Tigers, Red Wings, and Pistons. Hearns became the first fighter in history to win titles in five weight classes. Faygo signed the twenty-four-year-old one-punch knockout specialist to pitch Faygo punch. Advertising writer Betsey Hansell watched the photo session in a small east-side studio. Hearns' line was "Me and Faygo, we go back a long way." The campaign included three hundred billboards, in-store displays, and radio. Hansell wrote that Jackie Kallen, a former reporter and one of the few female promoters of boxing, helped prep Hearns for the shoot. He was baby-oiled to accentuate his muscles and spritzed to simulate sweat. Blue lights highlighted his hair, and white lights spotlighted the Faygo. Hansell quoted Kallen: "Faygo punch is a natural for Tommy. I hope everyone gets that connection." Kallen suggested, "Let's put Tommy in the ring and get this huge punching bag bottle of Faygo; Tommy could splatter it and say, 'It's a hit.'"

Faygo missed the boat as other bottlers' hydroplanes thundered on the Detroit River. Race boats included *Miss Towne Club*, several *Miss Pepsis*, *Miss Vernors*, and several *Miss Budweisers*.

Susie Feigenson liked the sports connections and told her father Faygo should bring in baseball Hall of Famer Darryl Strawberry to push Redpop. It did not happen. Another of her unused suggestions was that Faygo have its own boat in the annual Detroit hydroplane races. The event featured a *Miss Pepsi*, sponsored by Detroit's Pepsi-bottling Dossin family. The Dossin Great Lakes Museum on Belle Isle gets its name from the family and has the *Miss Pepsi* hydroplane as a featured attraction. Detroit's Towne Club pop company sponsored a boat, and so did Budweiser.

Faygo's TV presence dwindled in the 1980s, and it stayed away from TV campaigns for about five years until a modest 1992 campaign launching its cherry festival flavor, inspired by Michigan's cherry orchards in the state's northwestern Lower Peninsula. A greatly expanded distribution area, the expense of wide-area TV buys, and the affordability of new media meant Faygo's glory days in TV were over.

Genie out of the Bottle

Faygo's current promotional wave is tailored to web surfers and a national base of pop lovers. It uses social media, it has some sass, and it engages people in the conversation. It also has roots that go way back. With the Faygo Kid, Redpop, and the Boat Song, Faygo found a place in people's hearts, but those people were aging. By inviting younger people to engage with their friends around pop, Faygo gave up some control of its messaging. Engagement had been important to the Feigensons, whether that meant shipping people pop, practically giving away hit records, or inviting them to submit recipes. People became fondly loyal to their pop. Some expressed that at the store. Others expressed it by word of mouth. And a few leaped beyond. Once the genie was out of the bottle and people began crafting their own messages, Faygo could only stand by, watch, and hope for the best.

Historically, Faygo engaged its fans in several contests and collaborations. Susie Feigenson remembers when Faygo had a name-the-bunny contest and offered a big, stuffed-animal rabbit in a tuxedo to whoever could name it. She recalls that one child sent in scores of postcards. "'Name the rabbit Blackie.' 'Name the rabbit Whitey.' 'Name the rabbit Pinky.' The child obviously wanted that rabbit so much." Her father said, "Just send her the rabbit."

Faygo recipe collections, besides the one it partnered on with Weight Watchers, published hundreds of contributors' names over more than fifty years.

In 2000, Faygo ran a contest for a new centennial flavor. A Monroe, Michigan, mom won with blueberry cream, and Faygo put her photo on bottles. A 2007 design-a-flavor contest led to a rhubarb pie flavor. The flavors did not last, but their real value was in publicity and engagement.

Faygo's new advertising agency, the TMV Group, is inviting the youth market to engage friends, rather than drawing people in with seasoned celebs such as Fields, Karras, and Rivers. TMV asserts Faygo was "on the verge of losing its fizz with millennials" until the agency "made it come alive through social media via a new character, the Flavor Master, and on a new website aimed at entertaining as much as selling."

There are echoes of Faygo traditions in the new campaigns. Faygo's good-sport president, Al Chittaro, has gamely donned a nightcap, smoking jacket, and ascot to play the Flavor Master, reminiscent of when the company created the Faygo Kid and Herkimer Bottleneck characters. In character on YouTube, Chittaro said, "Normally, I just daydream of becoming a real-life Willy Wonka of pop, but today my mind drifted elsewhere. I dreamt of a Faygo Boat Song featuring you." The Flavor Master then instructed people on how to

FAYGO RECIPE BOOKS COOK UP ENGAGEMENT

1953: According to *100 Prize-Winning Recipes*, this book was organized in June 1951. Two years in the making, it was a response to "numerous telephone calls and letters reporting new and unusual dishes made with Faygo beverages." The recipes had a tie-in to early Faygo-sponsored TV shows, and weekly winners received seventeen-jewel Bulova watches. The sixteen-page guide included "Uptown Shrimp Sandwiches," "Faygo Tuna Fish Casserole," and "Faygo Black Cherry Harvard Beets." The book reported that these recipes and many others could be made with any of the eighteen Faygo flavors.

1965: *Faygo Award-Winning Diet Recipes.* This forty-page book contained fifty recipes for Faygo's seventeen sugar-free and diet flavors. The grand-prize winner was "Million Dollar French Dressing, made with Faygo diet ginger ale." First-prize winners included "Creamy Asparagus Cheese Salad Mold," "Low-Calorie Cola Coffee Shake," "Oven Beef Stew (a la sneaky)," and "Filet of Sole au Faygo." When the recipes came out, Faygo diet beverages were sweetened with cyclamates. A federal ban on the chemical in October 1969 forced pop makers to reformulate their diet drinks. Faygo was soon back on the market, sweetening diet pops

with saccharin. That affected the recipes, as aspartame does not heat as well.

1997: Celebrating 90 Years. This ninety-recipe collection began with special chef creations including "Faygo Crème Soda and Praline Bavarian with Faygo Orange Sauce and Creme Anglaise with Almond Cookies" by chef Philip Murray. The book concluded with a section called "Unusual Uses," which including using Faygo as bird-feeder nectar, bubble bath, bath crystals, and as a stain remover. The book, shaped like a can of pop, included recipes using both regular and diet Faygo flavors. The author of the award-winning recipe won a thousand dollars and a year's supply of Faygo.

2007: Centennial Recipe Book. This spiral-bound book had more than a hundred recipes from a "What's Your Recipe" contest and maintained the tradition of celebrity chefs and an expanded section of unusual uses. Recipes included "Faygo Twist of Cauliflower Soup," "Gingery Applesauce," "Chipotle Cherry Couscous," "Faygotastic Ribs," and "Send the Doctor Pork Chops," made with Dr Faygo pop, and a "Faygorita" grown-up beverage.

Faygo fans submitted thousands of recipes to win recognition and prizes with their creations. The completed books were sold at low prices, sometimes through labels on bottles of pop.

A New Yorker unused to Detroit's car culture, Norma Powell borrowed the loaner bicycles where she worked at Campbell Ewald downtown and rode them all around the city. She loved to ride those bicycles, but, in her heart, Norma wanted a bicycle of her very own. She was saving for a Faygo Redpop bicycle made at Detroit Bikes. Then, one day at a party, Campbell Ewald gave employees ten raffle tickets each to wager on tempting prizes. Norma put almost all her tickets on a brand-new Detroit Bikes bicycle. Although she says she never wins anything, Norma won the beautiful bicycle—a white one. So, she arranged for a trade with Detroit Bikes and began riding her new Redpop bike all around the city. She started taking pictures of Redpop on her travels, like this one by a mural on the Dequindre Cut Greenway, and posting them on Instagram as @redpopbike. As Norma and her bike became inseparable, people began recognizing them. One of her bosses said Norma should arrange a Redpop ridealong. Faygo started following @redpopbike. And Norma? She is planning more adventures on Redpop, whose sparkly paint reminds her of soda bubbles. *Photo credit: Norma Powell*

Norma Powell with the star of her @redpopbike
Instagram story. *Photo credit: Elmar Stewart*

record and email in their videos for a social media collaboration.

When Faygo launched its cotton candy pop in front of Detroit's WDIV-TV in 2014, Faygo marketing specialist Dawn Burch pushed the social media message: "We'll be rolling it out all summer, so we'll have events and samplings and contests and prizes, so make sure to follow us on Facebook and Twitter and Instagram."

Early in 2016, the company launched Faygo gold, a "rich, zippy" ginger ale that is found, of course, at the end of the rainbow of flavor. The launch featured a photo contest on Instagram with the person who captured the most Likes winning a "Pot of Gold," including Faygo gold pop, T-shirts, and a 24-karat gold bar from a local jeweler. Winners were announced on Instagram, Facebook, and Twitter.

In 2017 when it relaunched Arctic Sun, Faygo did it from inside its vault through a Facebook Live event with a trivia quiz and awarded prizes to people who answered questions online.

Street marketing Flavor Teams show up at community events to give away Faygo sips and swag. In 2017, the 110-year old company teased Facebook followers with a photo of a colorful birthday cake float being readied for Detroit's annual Thanksgiving Day parade, which broadcast as it rolls down Detroit's main street, Woodward Avenue. Call it street marketing or the world's largest Faygo float, it represented another new approach.

An upright piano painted in Faygo colors and rolled out onto downtown Detroit sidewalks spawned some impromptu entertainment from passersby. *Photo credit: Bill Yagerlener/Show Me Detroit Tours*

Who can resist a keyboard and a sunny day? *Photo credit: Bill Yagerlener/Show Me Detroit Tours*

Faygo's long history of saying "pop" in the face of people who want to call it "soda" went up a notch in 2017 with an online and billboard campaign orchestrated by the TMV Group. *Photo credit: Norma Powell*

The Michigan State University Marching Band's baritone members, known as "Hooahs," have several Faygo traditions. Besides playing the Faygo Boat Song around the stadium, members declare their favorite Faygo flavors and are gifted with a bottle when they join. *Photo credit: Rachel Sze*

Billboards, including Faygo's contrarian "Call It Pop" campaign, won recognition in the OBIES, the Outdoor Advertising Association of America's contest. #Callitpop billboards featured people's faces washed over in one color, such as Redpop, grape, and orange, like the face cans of the 1970s. This time, TMV used local models instead of stock photos from New York City. Rolling billboards on truck trailers, having graduated from paint to wraps, have won awards, too. Those twenty-four-foot-long bottles of pop were designed by TMV and installed by Mickey Truck Bodies and looked good enough to drink. Faygo ads also won in Detroit's D Show ad awards.

Family-founded Faygo has attracted musical families that are as different as they can be. One has been the Michigan State University Marching Band. Another was the rap duo Insane Clown Posse. The marching band came first. It has

been playing "Remember When You Were a Kid" at football games since the mid-1970s. In 2017, Matthew James recalled how he had arranged the tune "in the early seventies for my high school band. It was a hit! People would sway back and forth in the stands to its waltz feel and rhythm. I took it with me to MSU and, my freshman year, arranged it for the baritone section to play during the third quarter. Back then, the band would send sections out to go around the perimeter of the field and, during breaks in play, serenade the crowd during the third quarter. Every time we played 'Faygo,' each section of the stadium would sway as we played for them." James, department chair in performing arts at Lawrence Central High School in Indianapolis, recalled, "We played it for a halftime show in '77 or '78 and got the entire stadium swaying!" The song is still heard, in an original arrangement and an update, forty years later in practices, pop-ups around the 75,000-seat stadium, and by the alumni band. Faygo has cult status among the baritones, whose members receive a bottle of their favorite Faygo flavor when they join. Faygo encouraged the tradition by sending a big delivery truck and cases of pop in 1994 and again on September 24, 2016, for the fortieth anniversary of the tradition's debut.

Insane Clown Posse, whose recording label describes them as onetime "scrubs on the streets of Detroit," gets a more reserved reception from Faygo. The *New York Times* called this "one of the longest-running instances of an unsolicited celebrity endorsement." *Crain's Detroit Business* called it an "unsolicited sponsorship." The *Times* wrote that Matthew Rosenthal, head of marketing for Faygo, was "polite to a fault about I.C.P.," and said that the posse was a "big, influential" group that generated requests for Faygo when it played a new market. "We wish them the best," Rosenthal said, but on their lyrics alone, "they're not at all mainline kind of guys." Violent J and Shaggy 2 Dope grew up with Faygo. Now they tour with cannons, guns, and buckets to shower, shoot, spill, and spray Faygo on their Juggalo and Juggalette followers. They've been doing this since the early 1990s and learned to use diet because sugar can gum up sound boards and other electronics. Author Steve Miller said ICP sometimes travels with heaters to keep the pop warm and fizzy. They might spend twenty thousand dollars for a tour load and run through hundreds of liters of Faygo during the show. Loaders supplied with concert passes and

official-looking jumpsuits with the Faygo logo on the back help set up. The Posse is at the center of a network that includes Psychopathic Records ("The label that runs beneath the streets") and the underground music site Faygoluvers. Faygo is mentioned by a similar group, Twiztid. Detroit band Junk Food Junkies has tagged itself as "Faygo pop," but it is actually garage rock. It has recorded "Hot 'N' Ready," "Sugar High," "Fries Before Guys," and "Straight Faygo Klown'n." Gamzee, a character in the online webcomic *Homestuck*, also promotes Faygo in a way that is beyond the company's image and influence.

In a family-friendlier way, students in Susie Feigenson's 2001 high school English class got in on the make-your-own-message act. They had T-shirts printed up for themselves and their teacher with the distinctive Faygo crown-and-shield logo but the name "Feigo," a throwback to the founders and a tribute to a popular teacher.

POP Quiz

1. WHICH WAS NOT A FAYGO ADVERTISING LINE?

A. He went for Fayg-o-o-o
B. Too pooped to participate
C. Pop, pop, fizz, fizz
D. Rainbow of flavors
E. George Washington may have been the father of our country, but Faygo's the pop.

2. WHAT WAS FAYGO'S MASCOT?

A. Faygo the Clown
B. The Faygo Kid
C. A kangaroo named Faygo
D. A parrot that squawked "Faygo"

3. WHAT WAS BLACK BART TRYING TO TAKE FROM THE STAGECOACH?

A. The mail
B. A case of root beer
C. A maiden in distress
D. The horses

4. WHAT WAS NOT PROMOTED IN FAYGO RECIPE BOOKS AS AN "UNUSUAL USE"?

A. Carp bait
B. Doggie bones
C. Fabric dye
D. Stain remover
E. Shampoo

5. WHICH LINE DID JOAN RIVERS SAY IN A FAYGO DIET POP COMMERCIAL?

A. "At my age, a great evening is a Diet Faygo in a wineglass."
B. "We all mourn in our own way. I mourn with Diet Frosh."
C. "Why didn't they invent this fifty years ago when it could have helped me?"
D. "I love it. It's a proven fact: If I love it, it's fattening."

6. ONE OF THESE LINES DID NOT APPEAR ON STORE-DOOR OR SHELVING ADVERTISEMENTS. WHICH IS THE IMPOSTER?

A. Enlivens Playtime
B. Peps Up Party-Time
C. Refreshes TV-Time
D. Brightens Mealtime
E. Delicious Anytime

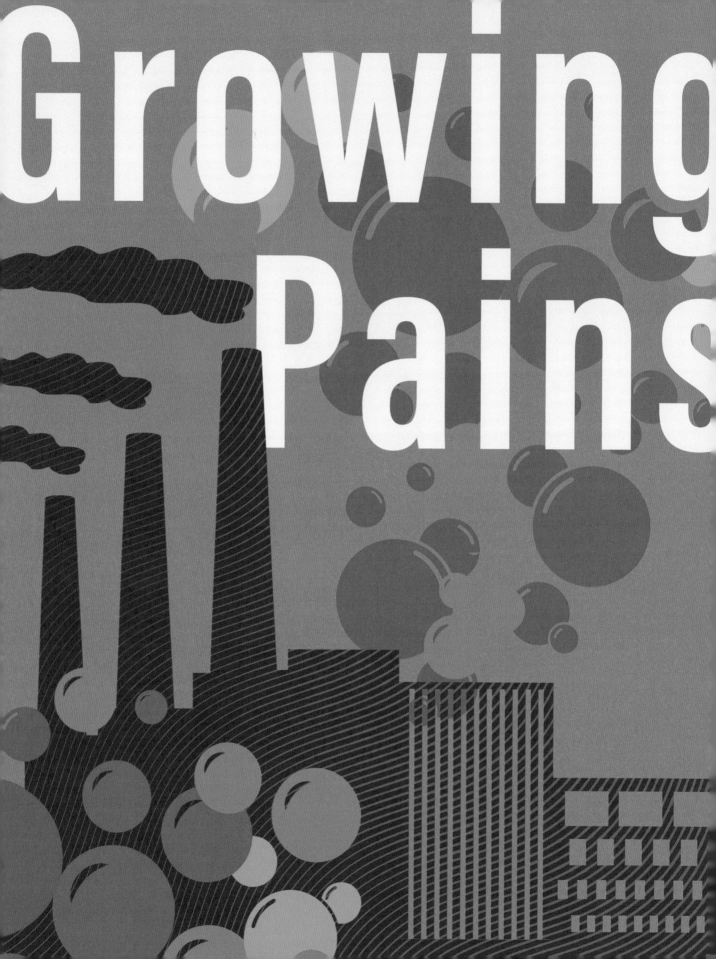

Crossroads

The second generation's innovations grew sales, but these changes were really just patches on a production site that dated to the horse-and-buggy days. What Faygo really needed was a whole new factory. In 1972, *Free Press* business writer Hugh McCann compared Mort Feigenson to a man with one foot on the dock and the other in a departing rowboat. Faygo had six acres but needed thirty, Mort estimated, and there was nothing like that available in Detroit. Faygo's approximately three hundred employees lived nearby. They walked, took the bus, or carpooled. Moving their jobs to the suburbs, with Detroit's creaky bus system, would cause major upheaval. Some would lose their jobs, and the Feigensons would lose a work-force admired for its loyalty and efficiency.

By then, five years after declaring it would reach beyond Michigan, Faygo was also sell-ing in Ohio, Indiana, and parts of New York,

Pennsylvania, Kentucky, and West Virginia. The Gratiot plant was supplying all of those areas from a sixty-five-year-old patchwork plant, largely cobbled together from other plants. Besides a new or expanded plant, Faygo needed a new business structure and new investment. In 1970, Faygo put an accountant and the head of the local Frank's Nursery and Sales on its board of directors. *Detroit News* financial editor Dennis Shere reported that before then, Mort, Phil, and Phil's mother, Celia, had made most of Faygo's big decisions in what he called "almost another family get-together." Shere predicted that the Feigensons' quest to be in every state east of the Mississippi would force them to surrender some control to get the capital they needed. Mort said Faygo needed a plant in the Detroit area capable of 50 million to 60 million cases a year, compared to its current 18 million cases, and that the plant would cost $5 million. The East Coast plant would need to be about a third that size, Mort told Shere, and would cost $1.5 million. Mort said the money could come from selling stock in the family-run company, or through a merger.

Mort spent most of 1972 looking for a site. He said he wanted to stay in Detroit but added, "I have the feeling that most people don't believe us. Anyone who says he wants to stay in the city . . . I mean, nobody's going to believe us." He esti-mated that cleared land in Detroit cost $40,000 to $60,000 an acre, while suburban land was $10,000 to $14,000 with all the amenities of roads and water. But cost aside, he could not find the land in Detroit. Faygo declined the city's offer of a parcel

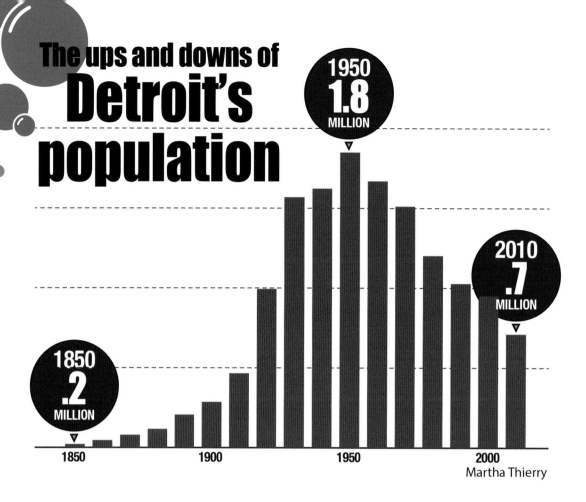

The ups and downs of Detroit's population

1850 .2 MILLION

1950 1.8 MILLION

2010 .7 MILLION

1850   1900   1950   2000

Martha Thierry

near Zug Island, a one-time dumping ground and steelmaking site, as unfit for bottling. Faygo was at a crossroads. Reporter McCann described the company's dilemma this way: "Should Faygo, which has done business in Detroit for 65 years and depended on an inner-city workforce, continue its traditional loyalty to its employee—and damn the consequences? Or should it commit to a suburban plant to pursue aggressively expanded markets and profits?"

From 1970 to 1980, Detroit lost three hundred thousand residents, the largest ten-year decline in its history. Although continuing population flight was draining Detroit, abandonment was dispersed. It pockmarked neighborhoods, and it hit the east side around Faygo hard, but it did

not clear out whole sections. Sometimes abandonment left solitary houses standing, as if on urban prairies. The days had not yet come when Detroit would consider closing parts of the city or assembling parcels that could become the urban farms of today.

Keeping Faygo in Detroit became an issue for Detroit's mayors. It was more than jobs and taxes. Detroit was also bleeding marquee businesses. Faygo was one of the few anchors on Detroit's faded east side and had grown from pop company to pop icon. By the summer of 1972, Berry Gordy had moved the last of Detroit's Motown studios to Los Angeles. In 1975, the Detroit Lions football team moved to the suburbs, and the Detroit Pistons basketball team followed in 1978. Also that year,

Vlasic, a Detroit pickle company for generations, was sold to Campbell Soup Co. In January 1983, Hudson's downtown department store, once the world's largest, closed.

At the same time, the bottling industry was consolidating around the Feigensons. "Detroit's Drink," Vernors, had a succession of owners starting in 1966, its hundredth anniversary. In 1985, United Brands closed Vernors' Woodward Avenue facility, moving production and three hundred jobs out of the city. That left Faygo as the last independent pop bottler in the city. Stroh, Faygo's east-side neighbor and partner in the bottle bill battle, was struggling and announced in 1985 it was closing its 135-year-old brewery. The next morning's front page of the *Detroit Free Press* said "Stroh won't brew here anymore" and showed a hangdog bartender at a beer tap.

Keeping Faygo in the city was top of mind at Detroit City Hall. In a February 1973, editorial, the *Detroit News* reported that Mayor Roman Gribbs was considering using eighty acres of the rundown Michigan State Fairgrounds for light industry. "Uppermost in his mind is the Faygo beverage firm, which is landlocked on its present eastside location and likely to build a new plant for its 300 employees in the suburbs," the paper said. In a July debate among mayoral candidates, one railed that "dumb . . . stubborn" city bureaucrats would end up "losing Faygo for Detroit by letting it go out to Southfield," in the suburbs.

For the winner of that election, Coleman A. Young, keeping Faygo also meant keeping it chilled. That came out in the *Detroit News'* June

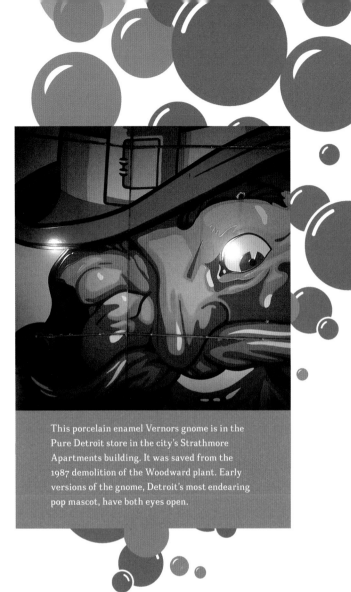

This porcelain enamel Vernors gnome is in the Pure Detroit store in the city's Strathmore Apartments building. It was saved from the 1987 demolition of the Woodward plant. Early versions of the gnome, Detroit's most endearing pop mascot, have both eyes open.

9, 1974, News Talk column, "assembled from items arriving from our reporters via a computerized typewriter that uses a TV screen instead of paper for writing and editing." The first item said:

Ex-Lion Alex Karras and Detroit's Mayor Young share a common taste. A neatly typed sign on the door of the refrigerator in the hallway down from Young's office reads, "Please be sure that there is always at least one cold Faygo redpop for the mayor." Another day, another sign: "Don't drink

There can hardly be a more literal use of the term "rebranding" than what Faygo did to transition straw-berry pop to Redpop.

this unless you're Coleman Young." Later that year, when asked about his choice in comfort foods, Young said, "My real craving after an illness is to get away from that junk they give you in hospitals and to get back to my usual unbalanced diet of things like meat and gravy and Faygo redpop."

In 1976, after Detroit city councilman Jack Kelley swore off alcohol, Faygo offered him a lifetime supply of Redpop, delivered by the case each Monday. Faygo also asked Kelley to serve as "Redpop Ambassador of the Year." Kelley said he didn't want Karras to think he had competition and added, "A donnybrook between two redpop drinkers would be ridiculous. Redpop with a drop of whiskey was one of my hangover cures in the old days. But now I know redpop is a lot better straight." In 1980, his five years of sobriety were celebrated with a billboard declaring him "Black Jack Kelley, the redpop champ."

So, what did Faygo do? To borrow a question from the Faygo Kid commercial, which way did they go, which way did they go? Did the Feigensons abandon the city, or give up on expanding? They did neither. A surprisalistic third option emerged.

The 1973 Arab oil crisis drove gasoline prices from 39 cents a gallon to an unheard-of 53 cents. Mort was plainly worried when he wrote to employees in that December's *Faygogazette*.

> Like you, I wonder how seriously my driving will be affected by the gasoline shortage; whether my house will be cold and uncomfortable before the winter sets in. In addition, I am concerned about our ability to keep the plant operating at full tilt next year. Will we be able to get the raw materials we need? Will we have the power to produce the product? Will we have the fuel to deliver to our customers throughout the Midwest? These are disturbing thoughts.

The following May, a small article in the *Detroit Free Press* said that Faygo would stay in Detroit: "All that consternation over the soda pop people moving out of the city can be put aside. But Faygo has several out-of-state markets. And given fuel supply uncertainties and rising costs, Faygo folks have decided to build satellite plants near those market areas to save gasoline." Worries about Faygo were eclipsed by worries about Detroit's car companies. Gas prices stayed high until 1986, and the furor about Faygo leaving the city disappeared in a murmur. But the silence was deceptive. Satellite plants would help Faygo with the one-two punch that was coming.

When the Feigensons broke ground on an addition that would bring jobs back from the suburbs, Detroit's Redpop-loving mayor, Coleman Young, pitched in. *From left*: Herman, Phil, and Mort Feigenson with Young. *Photo courtesy of the Feigenson family archives/Paul T. D'Aigle*

Going Once, Going Twice . . .

After telling *Forbes* in 1982 that the economy had "knocked the hell" out of Faygo, Mort fell uncharacteristically silent. The Faygo front man ducked behind the scenes to work on the company's biggest deal. Mort revealed in 1986, "We decided early on in 1983 that Faygo was not big enough to do what we wanted to do." As Faygo broke ground on a million-dollar, thirty-thousand-square-foot expansion that March, Mort was looking for a suitor, just as he had been looking for land in the 1970s. He found one. TreeSweet, the fruit juice marketing company, "came along and the fit looked pretty good," he said.

TreeSweet Companies was taken over in 1984 by former Coca-Cola executive Clinton E. Owens and a silent partner. Owens aspired to create a national food conglomerate, and in 1985 he acquired two General Foods frozen concentrate brands, Orange Plus and Awake, for $20 million. Owens told the *Chicago Tribune* that negotiations for Faygo, which was having a record year with

Detroit Free Press publisher David C. Lawrence Jr. sent this photo, taken the day Faygo said it would stay, to Mort Feigenson with a note of congratulations. The million-dollar, 30,000-square-foot addition brought 100 data, sales, and finance employees back into the city. That weekend, the paper published a profile of Feigenson. *Photo credit: David C. Turnley for the* Detroit Free Press

Johnnie Whitt works the line in Faygo's Gratiot plant. He and about 375 other employees went through their second takeover in fifteen months during May of 1987. *Photo credit: William Archie for the* Detroit Free Press

$105 million in sales in thirty-nine states, started that year. In February 1986, as the purchase was announced, Owens said TreeSweet could supply juices to Faygo, which would produce "juice-added" carbonated beverages. He said, "We think that such juice drinks can reach $12 billion to $15 billion in annual sales within 10 years," and predicted they would be 20 percent of the US soft drink market by 2006.

Mort attended the announcement, at which Owens said TreeSweet would keep Faygo's workers but not the Feigensons. Mort told the *Free Press* that the family decided to sell Faygo because it "couldn't do well unless it grew and became a stronger company" and that the sale was "the only way to go." The sale price was not disclosed. Susie Feigenson said her father, Philip, saw the sale as a way to provide for his sisters, Blanche, Ruth, and Gertrude. Susie said, "He breathed, ate and slept this business. It was tremendously hard for him to sell." But Phil was a businessman and stuck with what he knew. With all the trouble that sugar had caused Phil over the years, one might think he'd try something new. Instead, he started the Canadian Blending sugar company. Later, he got into a water company.

Soon, closed-door negotiations were happening again. In May 1987, National Beverage Corp. of Florida purchased Faygo from TreeSweet, which soon filed for bankruptcy reorganization and was sold. National Beverage brought with it a complicated origin that did not include any beverages. It was a holding company formed in 1985 and entered the beverage business when it bought Shasta Beverages from Sara Lee Foods. With Shasta headquartered in California and Faygo in Detroit, National Beverage had coast-to-coast coverage with plants near a dozen big cities. Formed by Nick A. Caporella, the aphorism-spouting billionaire son of a coal miner, National Beverage is the nation's fourth-largest beverage company. Its brands include Big Shot, Everfresh, and LaCroix.

For more than thirty years, National Beverage has kept its 1987 promise to keep Faygo in Detroit—and it left day-to-day operations in the hands of Sheridan, Lipsky, and Chittaro, who had learned directly from the Feigensons. Somehow, the Feigensons had sold Faygo to one company that held on just long enough to pass it on to another company that was just joining the beverage business.

Faygo and Mario? It was a thing in 1993. Faygo helped promote the Super Mario Brothers film with limited edition eight-ounce cans of Mario Punch, Princess Toadstool Cherry, Luigi Berry, and Yoshi Apple. Some regular Faygo cans and bottles also promoted the film. Social media bubbled in 2017 when Faygo teased on Instagram, "What would you say if we told you there was a Faygo Easter egg in the game that no one has found to this day?"

Faygo president Stan Sheridan said innovative flavors balanced with a core of consistent favorites was the way to go after the cola giants. *Photo credit: George Waldman for the* Detroit Free Press

The Soda Bubble

The drinks may be soft, but the business is hard.

After riding the soda bubble for a century, pop has come under pressure in the new millennium. Every year since the peak-volume year of 2004, soda pop sales in the United States have declined. Pop is getting squeezed in several ways.

More than a century of caution about sugar, let alone artificial sweeteners, is catching up. When the Feigensons turned from baking to bottling, Americans were consuming about forty-five pounds of sugar a year and using some

National Beverage brought Faygo in on its St. Nick's fundraiser for St. Jude Children's Research Hospital. Before Christmas, Faygo and Shasta have sold specially labeled flavors including candy cane cola, cranberry smash, and frosty red grape.

U.S. pop consumption down
In gallons, per capita

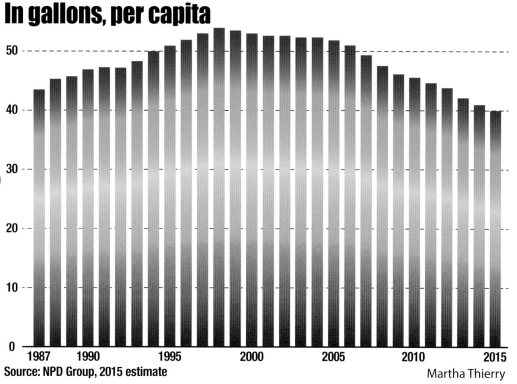

Source: NPD Group, 2015 estimate

Martha Thierry

Faygo hit the non-carbonated fruit drink market in a big way, launching many of its non-pop flavors at once. One advantage of leaving the bubbles out was that some returnable container laws included only carbonated beverages.

saccharin as a substitute. Even at that time, scientists began connecting excess sugar to diabetes and then Alzheimer's. Throughout the twentieth century, salt, fat, eggs, and other foods took turns as dietary bogeymen. By 2000, though, the medical community, the US government, and the UN's World Health Organization were all focused on excessive sugar consumption.

Throughout pop's boom century, several artificial sweeteners were tried, studied, regulated, and discarded. Nothing tastes just like sugar, and even sweeteners that came close carried health warnings of their own. High-fructose corn syrup, a natural product sometimes labeled as HFCS, was judged to be worse than sugar, and pop makers have touted their return to cane sugar.

With sugar demonized, especially when delivered in pop, the gates were open for the sin taxes long levied on alcohol and cigarettes. States and cities taxed sugar-sweetened pop by the ounce or when served in large amounts. But, like any tax, the pop penalty was not just about health. It was about raising money.

In 2016, voters made Philadelphia the first major city to charge a soda pop tax. They approved a tax of 1.5 cents per ounce, twenty-four times the state's tax on beer. The tax also was applied to diet pops, sport drinks, and teas. An estimated $91 million in revenue a year was to pay for early childhood education. That August, the Tax Foundation policy research organization judged Philly's pop tax to be a failure in improving health or raising money.

One analyst saw Philadelphia's soda tax as a boon for Faygo's parent, National Beverage Corp. The analyst noted a month after the tax took effect that the company's LaCroix beverages, with twenty flavors and about 25 percent of the carbonated water market, could gain more sales than it would lose from Faygo, Shasta, and its Rip It energy drinks. The analyst predicted big gains for National Beverage. In May 2017, the company was bubbly about the future of its unsweetened waters: "The release of our year-end financial statements certified that FY 2017 was the best year in the history of National Beverage—absolutely!" stated Caporella.

> Beating the estimates of both our fans and cash-poor detractors, and even our own "look-see" estimate, Team National posted industry-leading revenue and earnings growth. Our long-term shareholders also enjoyed another banner year; 90% price appreciation + $1.50 per share dividend paid + another $1.50 per share dividend payment on the way. There is

no doubt our exceptional financial results are the result of Team National's creativity combined with executing the right strategy. . . . This creativity is now also focused on Shasta Sparkling Water, our SDA (soft drink alternative) which features the industry's first "clean label." With the taste profile of a traditional soft drink in a "100% all-natural" beverage, the Shasta Sparkling Water line is targeted to those "crossover consumers" within the $81 billion US carbonated soft drink segment seeking guilt-free refreshment containing no calories, sodium or sweeteners.

A LaCroix sales dip in October 2017 had some analysts asking whether its bubble was bursting. Caporella took them to task in colorful fashion.

Another challenge has been consolidation. Of the several dozen bottlers on Detroit's east side, only Faygo remained. In 1988, the year after National Beverage bought Faygo, the Michigan Soft Drink Association reported its membership had dwindled from fifty to fifteen in twenty years.

Concerns about artificial sweeteners, sugar's role in diabetes and obesity, taxes, and growing suspicions about public drinking water supplies have pushed people's packaged beverage purchases toward water. In 2016, bottled water sales in the United States surpassed pop for the first time. Michael C. Bellas, chairman and CEO of the

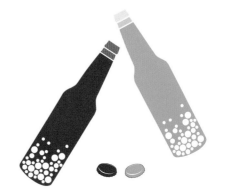

Faygo mixers have perked up sales around the holidays and won it recognition. When mixers were first packaged with smaller labels and white bottom cups to show off the purity of the product, the industry heralded the innovation.

Faygo's parent since 1987, National Beverage Corp., has 25 percent of the growing market for flavored sparkling water. That could be a hedge for Faygo in the decline of pop sales, which began in 2004.

New York–based Beverage Marketing Corporation, said, "When Perrier first entered the country in the 1970s, few would have predicted the heights to which bottled water would eventually climb. Where once it would have been unimaginable to see Americans walking down the street carrying plastic bottles of water, or driving around with them in their cars' cup holders, now that's the norm."

Warehouse deliveries, which Mort called a game changer, became a hang-up when some chains decided they would rather handle just their house brands, forcing Faygo back to convenience stores and gasoline stations.

What will the soda bubble mean for Faygo?

It could depend on how much Faygo's history of quality and innovation help it in today's craft-pop market, and it could depend on what happens with its parent company. Faygo responded to health concerns with a line of diet pops, promoted them heavily, and quickly reformulated the line when cyclamates were banned. It developed a line of unsweetened mixers. It listens to its fan base. Faygo has innovated manufacturing, packaging, and delivery systems to grow market share. Faygo stood by people when others would not, and it engendered loyalty. Philip H. Howard, an associate professor at Michigan State University, studies food industry ownership. He observes that, despite the impression of diversity given by a large number of soft drink choices, a small number of companies own most of the brands. They tend to swallow competitors. The same thing is happening in bottled water. Faygo's parent company is not small but would seem to be an attractive purchase for giants Coke, Pepsi, and now Nestlé Waters.

Susie Feigenson said, "Certainly the industry has had enormous challenges—the Teamsters, sugar, artificial sweeteners, the bottle law. There was always one hurdle after another." Faygo's future will come down to how well National Beverage Corp.—or a successor—lets Faygo be Faygo.

1. WHICH IS THE REAL STOCK MARKET SYMBOL FOR NATIONAL BEVERAGE CORP.?

A. POPS
B. NBC
C. FIZZ
D. BEV
E. BURP

2. WHAT CHARITY DO SPECIAL ST. NICK'S FLAVORS BENEFIT?

A. St. Jude Children's Research Hospital
B. Feed the Children
C. Salvation Army
D. The Old Newsboys
E. Gleaners

3. HOW LONG DID TREESWEET OWN FAYGO BEFORE SELLING IT TO NATIONAL BEVERAGE?

A. 15 minutes
B. 15 days
C. 15 weeks
D. 15 months
E. 15 years

4. WHICH BEVERAGE IS NOT ONE OF FAYGO'S COUSINS UNDER THE NATIONAL BEVERAGE BANNER?

A. Shasta
B. Nehi
C. Everfresh
D. LaCroix

5. FAYGO HAD A CAMEO IN THE MOVIE:

A. 8 Mile
B. Grosse Pointe Blank
C. RoboCop
D. Beverly Hills Cop II

6. WHICH DISH WAS NOT SERVED AT THE "TASTE OF FAYGO" IN THE POP-UP RESTAURANT POP ABOVE DETROIT'S CHECKER BAR?

A. Black cherry wild boar kabobs
B. Just Peachy Michigan salad with peach Faygo vinaigrette
C. Grilled swordfish with pineapple watermelon Faygo salsa
D. Orange-glazed Faygo Kid lamb cutlets

CORRECT ANSWERS: 1-C; 2-A; 3-D; 4-B; 5-B; 6-D

1882
Perry Feigenson born in Russia.

1884
Ben Feigenson born in Russia.

1901
Perry arrives in Cleveland at age 19 and gets a job in a bakery.

1905
Perry moves to Detroit and opens a bakery at 498 St. Antoine Street between Division and Alfred.

1907
Perry and Ben rent a house at Benton near Hastings in Detroit and turn part of it into a bottling shop. They live upstairs and deliver with a horse-drawn wagon. The address is given as 118 Benton in the 1908 city directory and as 507 Hastings in a 1911 newspaper ad.

1910
Despite starting up in a financial panic, the brothers are successful enough in a couple years to tear down the house, build a larger plant, and hire six employees.

1912
Horses get a break as the brothers invest in a brand-new GMC truck. Perry buys a Ford Model T for himself.

1920
The Feigensons open a new bottling plant in August. It is on Beaubien Street at Erskine. The Feigensons say the plant can clean and fill 75,000 small pop bottles a day. They have 30 employees and 12 trucks. The name "Faygo," with a logo, appears in an ad in the October 29 *Detroit Jewish Chronicle*. The ad lists a dozen flavors.

1956
"The Faygo Kid" commercial airs.

1964
Perry Feigenson dies in January at age 81.

1965
Faygo begins advertising during televised Detroit Tigers baseball games.

1966
Harvey Lipsky becomes vice president.

1969
The US Food and Drug Administration bans cyclamates. Faygo quickly reformulates its low-calorie pops.

1973
The Faygo Boat Song commercial with "Remember When You Were a Kid" is recorded.

1974
Stan Sheridan is named chief financial officer.

1976
Michigan voters pass a law requiring a deposit on carbonated beverage bottles and cans.

Timeline

1926 — The company has 16 trucks and more than 40 employees.

1930–1931 — The early days of the Depression force Faygo to lay off people and cut production.

1934 — With Prohibition over and their drivers delivering pop at a number of saloons, the Feigensons consider adding beer but decide to stick with pop.

1934 — Faygo signs a $2,000 advertising contract with Julian Grace.

1935 — The plant on Beaubien is seized to make way for the Brewster-Douglass public housing projects, and Faygo gambles on a much larger building at 3579 Gratiot Avenue.

1938 — Faygo employs 75 people and has 25 trucks.

1946 — The next generation joins the company after World War II: Ben's son Philip and Perry's sons Mort and Herman.

1947 — Albert Feigenson dies at age 28.

1948 — Ben Feigenson dies.

1986 — TreeSweet Companies of Houston buys Faygo.

1987 — National Beverage Corp. of Florida acquires Faygo from TreeSweet.

1988 — National Beverage names Sheridan as Faygo president. He later joins the board.

1994 — Mort Feigenson dies on September 11.

2001 — Herman Feigenson dies on August 13.

2007 — Philip Feigenson dies on May 6.

2009 — *Bon Appétit* magazine designates Faygo root beer as one of the best root beers in America.

2011 — Faygo launches its first non-carbonated soft drinks and calls them "Ohana," Hawaiian for family. Serious Eats declares Faygo orange as "favorite orange" pop.

2016 — Al Chittaro is named president.

Faygo
Flavors

In the kid-classic 1970s Faygo commercial, a little boy tells the grocer he would like a Faygo. The grocer asks, "What flavor would you like?" The boy replies, "What flavors ya got?" The grocer runs out of breath listing flavors. Trying to list Faygo's flavors is exasperating. It is long and bedeviled by hits, flops, rebranding, and pops that were discontinued only to be revived later, sometimes with new names. Strawberry, one of Faygo's original three, was renamed Redpop to great success. Another early flavor, sassafras, became root beer. Root beers were also called draft root beer, draft-style root beer, big draft root beer, old-fashioned draft-style root beer, diet Western-style root beer, and old-fashioned root beer. How many is that? Also, some Faygo flavors are available only in certain regions. Flavors have been reformulated to suit changing regulations and tastes. A chronological list would be impossible. Consider that Arctic Sun, introduced in the 1990s, was discontinued and then re-released in 2017 for Faygo's 110th anniversary. Furthermore, some people have mistaken beverages by other companies to be Faygo creations. If you count the diet flavors, the special flavors, and all those root beers, the list is well more than one hundred. Consider this to be partial. The asterisks indicate flavors also available in diet.

60/40 (grapefruit/lime)*
Ace Hy
Apple cider
Arctic Sun
Birch beer
Black cherry
Black raspberry*
Bright (lemon & lime)
Candy apple
Centennial soda (blueberry cream for Faygo's
    hundredth in 2007)
Chateau Valley grape*
Chateaux Faygeaux
Cheri very cherry cola
Cherry
Cherry cola
Cherry festival
Chocolate treat
Cocoa cream soda
Cola*
Cotton candy
Creme soda*
Diet Bavarian creme soda
Diet Caribbean cola
Diet cherry-berry
Diet chocolate cream pie
Diet coconut cream
Diet Danish-style cherry with strawberry
Diet English ginger ale
Diet Frosh
Diet passion fruit punch
Diet raspberry creme
Diet strawberry-cherry
Diet wild strawberry
Double cola
Dr Faygo (originally Dr Mort)
Dry ginger ale
Dutch crème soda
Eve (apple)
Extra dry ginger ale
Faygo Bräu
Fruit punch
Ginger ale*

Ginger beer
Gold
Gold port
Golden ginger ale
Grape*
Grapefruit soda
Honeydew mist
Jazzin' blues berry
Key lime pie*
Kiwi strawberry
Lemon
Lemon-lime*
Lime rickey
Lithiated lemon
Mandarin orange
Moon Mist blue*
Moon Mist green* (similar to Mountain Dew
    and Mello Yello)
Moon Mist red* (also called Morning Mist)
Moonshine (similar to Mountain Dew)
North Bay dry ginger ale
Oasis punch
Orange*
Peach*
Pineapple
Pineapple orange*
Pineapple watermelon
Raspberry blueberry*
Redpop*
Redpop with lemon
Rhubarb pie (2007 "Design a Flavor" winner)
Rock & Rye* (also labeled as a crème cola)
Root beer* (diet Western-style root beer,
    old-fashioned root beer, old-fashioned
    draft-style root beer, draft root beer, draft-
    style root beer, big draft root beer)
Sassafras
Sensation*
Strawberry*
Tang-o (grapefruit)
Twist* (lemon-lime)
Uptown
Vanilla Creme Soda*

Ohana non-carbonated drinks

Blueberry lemonade
Cherry grapefruit
Citrus green tea
Kiwi strawberry
Lemon iced tea
Lemonade
Lemonade and iced tea
Mango
Mardi Gras pineapple orange
Melon
Original punch
Peach iced tea
Peach melon
Pineapple orange
Pink lemonade
Punch
Raspberry iced tea
Raspberry lemonade
Strawberry banana
Sweet tea

Tonic and sparkling waters

Club soda
Gini (bitter lemon) tonic
India Express quinine water
India Express tonic water
Sparkling cherry
Sparkling grapefruit
Sparkling lemon lime
Sparkling orange
Sparkling raspberry
Sparkling water
Tonic water*

St. Nick's flavors, also produced by National Beverage's Shasta, benefit St. Jude Children's Hospital around Christmas

St. Nick's candy cane cola
St. Nick's cranberry smash
St. Nick's frosty red grape
St. Nick's holiday punch
St. Nick's snowflake orange creme

Nintendo flavors, for a 1993 promotional campaign

Luigi Berry
Mario punch
Princess Toadstool cherry
Yoshi apple

Tradewinds teas and lemonades

Blueberry lemonade
Cherry grapefruit
Citrus green tea
Kiwi strawberry
Lemonade
Lemonade and iced tea
Mango
Melon
Original punch
Peach iced tea
Peach melon
Peach pineapple
Pineapple orange
Pink grapefruit diet
Pink lemonade
Raspberry iced tea
Raspberry lemonade
Strawberry banana
Sweet tea

Sources

Books

Abraham, Adam. *When Magoo Flew: The Rise and Fall of Animation Studio UPA.* Middletown, CT: Wesleyan University Press, 2012.

Allen, Frederick. *Secret Formula: The Inside Story of How Coca-Cola Became the Best-Known Brand in the World.* New York: Open Road Integrated Media (reprint), 2015.

Amidi, Amid. *Cartoon Modern: Style and Design in Fifties Animation.* San Francisco: Chronicle Books, 2006.

Austin, Dan. *Greetings from Detroit: Historic Postcards from the Motor City.* Detroit: Wayne State University Press, 2017.

Bolkosky, Sidney. *Harmony & Dissonance: Voices of Jewish Identity in Detroit, 1914–1967.* Detroit: Wayne State University Press, 1991.

Castelnero, Gordon. *TV Land Detroit.* Ann Arbor: University of Michigan Press, 2006.

"Cream Soda (A drink for summer in accordance with the Maine Law)." *Michigan Farmer* (1852): 183.

Finch, Christopher. *Of Muppets and Men: The Making of the Muppet Show.* New York: Muppet Press/Alfred A. Knopf, 1981.

Flinn, Gary. *Remembering Flint, Michigan: Stories from the Vehicle City.* Mount Pleasant, SC: Arcadia Publishing, 2010.

Harrigan, Patrick Joseph. *The Detroit Tigers: Club and Community, 1945–1995.* Toronto: University of Toronto Press, 1997.

Howard, Philip H. *Concentration and Power in the Food System: Who Controls What We Eat?* (Contemporary Food Studies: Economy, Culture and Politics). New York: Bloomsbury Academic, 2016.

Kiska, Tim. *From Soupy to Nuts: A History of Detroit Television.* Troy, MI: Momentum Books, 2005.

McDonough, John and Karen Egolf. *The Advertising Age Encyclopedia of Advertising.* Oxford, UK: Taylor & Francis, 2002.

McMahan, Harry Wayne. *The Television Commercial: How to Create and Produce Effective TV Advertising.* New York: Hastings House, 1954.

Miller, Steve. *Juggalo: Insane Clown Posse and the World They Made.* Boston: Da Capo Press, 2016.

Pendergrast, Mark. *For God, Country and Coca-Cola.* New York: Charles Scribner's Sons, 1993.

Rouch, Lawrence. *The Vernor's Story: From Gnomes to Now.* Ann Arbor: University of Michigan Press, 2003.

Schutt, Stefan, Sam Roberts, and Leanne White. *Advertising and Public Memory: Social, Cultural and Historical Perspectives on Ghost Signs.* New York: Routledge, 2017.

Shea, Stuart and Gary Gillette. *Calling the Game: Baseball Broadcasting from 1920 to the Present.* Phoenix: Society for American Baseball Research, 2015.

Sugrue, Thomas. *The Origins of the Urban Crisis: Race and Inequality in Postwar Detroit.* Princeton: Princeton University Press, 2014.

Wunderlich, Keith. *Vernor's Ginger Ale.* Mount Pleasant, SC: Arcadia Press (Images of America: Michigan), 2008.

Magazines, Newspapers, Journals

Acosta, Roberto. "No jail time for Michigan man in bottle return scam, report says." *MLive*, November 10, 2016.

Advertisement. "Ridiculous. If Proposal 'A' passes we'll be forced to charge you a deposit on cans as well as bottles." *Cass City Chronicle*, October 28, 1976.

"Alleged sugar 'fence' on trial." *Detroit Free Press*, April 12, 1924.

Angelo, Frank. "The cousins Feigenson: And that's how they make Faygo." *Detroit Free Press*, October 3, 1977.

Bascom, Lionel. "Faygo may start disposable bottle plant elsewhere." *Detroit Free Press*, October 12, 1976.

Beltaire, Mark, "Pop bottle treasure." *The Detroit News*, February 4, 1967.

Bennes, Ross. "Sex, drugs and Rock-n-Rye: An, uh, unsolicited sponsorship shakes up a spurt in growth at Faygo." *Crain's Detroit Business*, August 30, 2013.

"Big firms swallow up bottlers." *Chicago Tribune*, February 7, 1988.

"Bottleneck! Millions of missing bottles cause a pop crisis." *Detroit Free Press*, January 25, 1967.

Braunstein, Janet. "Faygo to tap interest in video game." *Detroit Free Press*, May 15, 1993.

Coffee, Gertha. "Faygo to launch marketing drive." *Detroit Free Press*, January 28, 1988.

"Criticism forces bottlers to battle throwaway litter." *Detroit Free Press*, July 8, 1966.

Crump, Constance. "Way to go, Faygo." *Crain's Detroit Business*, March 9, 1992.

Deck, Cecilia. "Faygo launches Michigan Cherry Festival with its first TV campaign in about five years." *Detroit Free Press*, March 6, 1992.

Deierlein, Robert, "The Mouse That Roared: Taking a Different Approach in Many Areas Pays off for Faygo." *Beverage World*, May 1990.

Detroit Free Press ad in support of bottle deposits. May 21, 1928.

Dewey, Caitlin. "Why Chicago's soda tax fizzled after two months—and what it means for the anti-soda movement." *The Washington Post*, October 10, 2017.

Eichenwald, Kurt. "Soda, the Life of the Party." *The New York Times*, July 16, 1985.

Elliott, Stuart. "Faygo's phasing out faces." *Detroit Free Press*, July 31, 1979.

"Faygo: Bottle bill cut profits by half." *Detroit Free Press*, February 28, 1980.

"Faygo going strong in 50th year." *American Soft Drink Journal* 107, no. 693 (September 1958): 20–22.

"Fifty years ago: Two-for-nickel pop gave Faygo start." *Detroit Free Press*, July 13, 1958.

"The Fox of the after-dinner circuit: Ahhh, yesss, Karrell Fox, good businessman, know him well." *Detroit Free Press*, March 2, 1975.

Gainor, Paul. "Faygo and Doner end long-standing ad ties." *The Detroit News*, January 22, 1976.

Gainor, Paul. "Faygo goes for new image." *The Detroit News*, August 12, 1976.

Goldstein, Richard. "Billy Rogell is dead at 98; star shortstop in the 1930s." *The New York Times*, August 13, 2003.

Haldane, Neal. "Faygo brings back glass bottles for pop." *The Detroit News*, June 5, 2001.

Hansell, Betsey. "Back to Detroit: Faygo will move Ferndale employees into new addition." *Detroit Free Press*, March 2, 1983.

Hansell, Betsey. "Hearns looks for a hit in Billboard Jungle." *Detroit Free Press*, March 7, 1983.

Hansell, Betsey. "Profile: Mort Feigenson, president, Faygo Beverages Inc." *Detroit Free Press*, March 7, 1983.

Hayden, Nicole. "Former Goldie's Pawn Shop mural to be covered." *Port Huron Times-Herald*, October 31, 2016.

Hopgood, Mei-Ling. "Former Faygo president was a booster of Detroit." *Detroit Free Press*, September 12, 1994.

Hunter, George, "Flavors, prices give Faygo an edge in a glutted market." *The Detroit News*, August 28, 1997.

Jones, Phillip M. "Faygo supports young scholars." *Michigan Chronicle*, June 5, 2002.

Jørgensen, Finn Arne. "A pocket history of bottle recycling." *The Atlantic*, February 27, 2013.

King, R. J. "Get Your Red Pop! The Flavor Master takes the world by storm." *DBusiness*, November/December 2012.

Klement, David. "Faygo ads remove diet pop from limbo." *Detroit Free Press*, August 14, 1973.

Kosoff, Maya. "Billionaire LaCroix C.E.O. attacks seltzer skeptics in all-caps rant." *Vanity Fair*, October 20, 2017.

Kraus, Robert. "Cyclamate ban stirs 'panic.'" *Detroit Free Press*, October 22, 1969.

Krebs, Michelle L. "Faygo unveils new $4.5 million system." *The Oakland Press*, May 11, 1983.

Lacy, Eric. "Future of Insane Clown Posse, Lansing unclear." *Lansing State Journal*, June 21, 2016.

Lazarus, George. "TreeSweet buys soft-drink firm." *Chicago Tribune*, February 19, 1986.

Malcolm, Hadley. "Bottled water about to beat soda as most consumed beverage." *USA Today*, June 8, 2016.

"Manufacturer is exonerated: Federal court clears name of Perry Feigenson, who was unjustly convicted." *Detroit Free Press*, June 1, 1924.

McCann, Hugh. "Faygo in dilemma as deadline nears." *Detroit Free Press*, October 1, 1972.

McCann, Hugh. "Faygo still undecided on public stock offering." *Detroit Free Press*, September 16, 1969.

McDonough, John. "W. B. Doner: 60th anniversary: Shop's 'vest-pocket' origins lead to billings of a half-billion dollars." *Advertising Age*, March 3, 1997.

Menard, Joe. "Philip Jerome Feigenson, Detroit Faygo executive's compassion popular with workers." *The Detroit News*, May 19, 2007.

Miro, Marsha. "Gallery owner gave city artists 'a home for their work.'" *Detroit Free Press*, September 21, 1984.

Myers, Tish. "Faygo story—it's never lost its fizz." *The Detroit News*, March 1, 1972.

Newman, Kara. "Rock and Rye: Good medicine."

Bon Appétit, November 26, 2012.

"New site rejected by Faygo." *Detroit Free Press*, April 11, 1972.

"New trial won by Feigenson." *Detroit Free Press*, May 11, 1924.

Noble, William T. "From the Detroit hangout of the Faygo kids." *The Detroit News Sunday Magazine*, October 5, 1969.

Nosowitz, Dan. "Why is cream soda called cream anyway?" *Bon Appétit*, March 9, 2017.

Oppedahl, John. "Faygo looking to suburbs for a cheaper site." *Detroit Free Press*, January 13, 1972.

Orr, Ralph. "Nobody sees red over Faygo worker gripes." *Detroit Free Press*, March 25, 1978.

Ostmann Jr., Robert. "Stroh, Faygo urge council not to back bottle measure." *Detroit Free Press*, October 29, 1976.

Ratliff, Rick. "W. B. Doner builds on 50 years of ideas." *Detroit Free Press*, February 23, 1987.

"Red pop for me." *Grosse Pointe News*, July 18, 1985.

Reiter, John. "Faygo ads ignore taboo; sales soar." *Detroit Free Press*, October 24, 1967.

Reiter, John. "Integration item: Thirst; Negro trade wooed." *Detroit Free Press*, August 20, 1968.

Reiter, John. "Soft drink sales set back by riots." *Detroit Free Press*, August 30, 1967.

"Revised strategy: Stay alive or dive were Faygo's options." *Michigan Business*, December 1986.

"Rival bakers in stew over bread." *Detroit Free Press*, October 16, 1906.

Rudolph, Barbara. "Bottle scars." *Forbes*, February 15, 1982.

Saunders, John. "Faygo changes hands once more, will maintain Detroit operations." *Detroit Free Press*, May 21, 1987.

Scott, Vernon. "Alex sells 'sugarless froshted frost.'" *United Press International*, December 30, 1973.

Shere, Dennis. "Faygo to have growing pains." *The Detroit News*, June 13, 1971.

Skid, Nathan. "Just Baked CEO sees revenue fizz with Faygo cupcakes." *Crain's Detroit Business*, November 18, 2010.

Skwira, Gregory. "Passover pop: Now that's kosher." *Detroit Free Press*, February 16, 1975.

Smith, Joel. "Faygo Celebrates 100th birthday." *The Detroit News*, March 2, 2007.

Smith, Leanne. "Peek through time: Foote & Jenks' flavor empire started with small store in Jackson." *Jackson Citizen-Patriot/MLive*, September 10, 2011

Smith, Ryan E. "Faygo: The Detroit pop company celebrates 100 years of fizz." *Toledo Blade*, November 2, 2007.

Stearns, Patty LaNoue. "Faygo flavor wizard helps Detroit's historic pop bottler create the fizz of the future." *Detroit Free Press*, August 30, 1995.

Stopa, Marsh. "Faygo seeks site in city for new plant." *Crain's Detroit Business*, August 4, 1997.

"Sugar suit caused by war is settled." *Detroit Free*

Press, March 12, 1915.

Talbert, Bob. "Elusive voice of W. C. Fields." *Detroit Free Press*, August 19, 1968.

The American Bottler, January 1, 1915.

"They built wintertime volume." Bottler Briefs, Glass Container Manufacturers Institute, November 1966.

Thompson, Ken. "Faygo plans new expansion on crest of growing market." *Detroit Free Press*. January 16, 1966.

Vlasic, Bill. "Faygo to stay put: New owner to give U.S. a taste of Detroit." *The Detroit News*, May 11, 1987.

Von Schneidemesser, Luanne. "Soda or pop?" *Journal of English Linguistics* 24, no. 4 (December 1996).

Walker, Rob. "Celebrity Sweepstakes." *The New York Times Magazine*, August 27, 2010.

Walsh, Tom, "Beyond Rock & Rye and a hard place: Faygo Chugs Along." *Detroit Free Press*, October 10, 2002.

Weeks, George. "Bottle bill a success in Michigan." *Traverse City Record-Eagle*, April 30, 2017.

Wegener, Margaret. "Pop shop family won name game in 1885 Detroit." *Detroit Free Press*, May 7, 1992.

Werner, Larry. "Battle goes on as the bottle law nears birthday." *Detroit Free Press*, November 29, 1979.

Wernle, Bradford. "Quick moves make Faygo a pop star." *Crain's Detroit Business*, September 20, 1993.

White, George. "Houston-based TreeSweet purchases Faygo." *Detroit Free Press*, February 19, 1986.

Zuchino, David. "How will consumers handle the returnables?" *Detroit Free Press*, November 26, 1978.

Websites

Detroitkidshow.com

Earl Klein Biography. Accessed February 15, 2018. http://www.earlklein.com/earl-klein-biography.

Golick, Ed. "Karrell Fox—the King of Korn." Accessed September 17, 2017. http://detroitkidshow.com/Karrell_Fox.htm.

Golick, Ed. "Which way did he go? The true story of the Faygo Kid." Accessed September 17, 2017. http://www.detroitkidshow.com/The_Faygo_Kid.htm.

Faygo.com

Funding Universe. "Faygo Beverages, Inc., history." Accessed February 24, 2018. http://www.fundinguniverse.com/company-histories/faygo-beverages-inc-history/.

Mark, Florine. Accessed February 15, 2018. http://www.michiganwomenshalloffame.org/Images/Mark,%20Florine.pdf

Sullivan, Jack. "Nathan Van Beil and His Rock'n Rye Trials of 1880." April 1, 2015. Accessed September 16, 2017. http://pre-prowhiskey-men.blogspot.com/2015/04/nathan-van-beil-and-his-rockn-rye.html.

Uhle, Frank. W. B. Doner & Co. Accessed February 15, 2018. http://www.encyclopedia.com/books/politics-and-business-magazines/wb-doner-co.

Yau, Nathan. "Pseudo-variety and ownership of the soft drink industry." FlowingData.com. Accessed December 13, 2017. https://flowingdata.com/2010/08/23/pseudo-variety-and-ownership-of-the-soft-drink-industry/.

Unpublished Manuscripts

"History of Faygo Beverage Company." James F. Chapman, Inc. Circa 1958. Based on an interview with Perry Feigenson when he was 77.

Rosenthal, Matt. "Sweet, Fizzy and Full of Flavor: Faygo Celebrates 90 Years." March 14, 1997 release.

TV Commercials and Videos

Some of the most engaging parts of the Faygo story are told in its TV commercials and videos. It is worth the time to watch these online. (All accessed at these web addresses on June 9, 2018.)

Commercials

Herkimer Bottleneck for Uptown
https://youtu.be/ZW4U_ABBY1A

Uptown Soda, 1955
https://youtu.be/4Go2zyzcMQo

Jim Henson Commercial for Faygo
https://youtu.be/PxQvW7NNmno

The Faygo Kid
https://youtu.be/MPtenJvEYCA

Faygo Black Cherry
https://youtu.be/q62zBY6lMlA

Faygo Boat Song
https://youtu.be/LQqyDj7RX6Y

Faygo Boat Song (music and lyrics only)
https://youtu.be/o1ppc4KIKNE

Joan Rivers in Restaurant for Faygo Diet Root Beer
https://youtu.be/7xtDOBe5LSk

Joan Rivers with Paula Warner at Pool for Faygo
    Diet Frosh
https://youtu.be/a8lmW4oB3yI

Alex Karras for Sugar-free Redpop
https://youtu.be/MBY9SwbhXgA

What Flavors Ya Got? One-Calorie Version
https://youtu.be/JYNXHPkCe3I

What Flavors Ya Got? Laurel And Hardy Version
https://youtu.be/6VRdc-bUxwo

Redpop Commercial with Jamie Farr
https://youtu.be/nDefpGQcM7g

Monkey Business (Shot at Detroit Zoo)
https://youtu.be/l3rTzAkQ1RI

Rainbow of Flavors (Paint Roller Version)
https://youtu.be/JWjtLJNiPxE

Rainbow of Flavors (Dance Party Version)
https://youtu.be/8VDnR2v2q4A

Faygo Baseball Song (2011 TMV Group Audio)
https://youtu.be/LLoMBj19JXU

Diet Faygo with Pies
https://youtu.be/7P4d5SqPkU4

Costume Party
https://youtu.be/KnzonffqUBo

More Videos
Faygo Factory Tours
(Produced for Faygo in 2011 by the TMV Group)
https://youtu.be/VMfdnGox6Xk
(With parts of classic commercials)
https://youtu.be/UBAeXETg-3o

Faygo History by Wayne State University
https://youtu.be/AaXsTmvoQUk

Faygo History by WXYZ-TV Detroit
https://youtu.be/dYE_8XheKdo

Faygo Launches Cotton Candy Flavor, WDIV-TV
    Detroit
https://www.clickondetroit.com/consumer/faygo-
    unveils-new-cotton-candy-pop-on-local-4

Faygo Sites
YouTube channel: https://www.youtube.com/
    channel/UCnr--JMAZS-_2nZXovuZD_g/videos
http://faygounbottled.com/
http://callitpop.com

Michigan State Marching Band Playing "Remem-
    ber When You Were a Kid"
https://www.youtube.com/watch?v=hA-
    C79yzG9Fo

PopUmentary Faygo History and Plant Tour
https://youtu.be/OLbW_sl-uuI
https://vimeo.com/104406859

About the
Author

Joe Grimm wrote *The Faygo Book* after building up a tremendous thirst working on *Coney Detroit* with Katherine Yung (Wayne State University Press, 2012). A lifelong Detroit-area resident and twenty-five-year veteran of the *Detroit Free Press*, Grimm is a Michigan State University journalism professor. His favorite Faygo flavor is Rock & Rye.